✓

76

Ross Williamson, Hugh, 1901-
    Paris is worth a Mass. N.Y., St. Martin's
Press [c1971]

    I.t.

        x Williamson, Hugh Ross

'PARIS IS WORTH A MASS'

HUGH ROSS WILLIAMSON

Paris is worth a Mass

ST. MARTIN'S PRESS
NEW YORK

To
Douglas Rossdale

CONTENTS

7

Assassination is the extreme form of censorship

GEORGE BERNARD SHAW

I

The Cardinal de Bourbon

The death of 'Monsieur', King Henri III's brother, and heir to the throne of France, raised graver problems than even his dedicated talent for mischief-making had achieved in his lifetime. It left the Huguenot Henry of Navarre next in succession to the crown. As matters stood in that summer of 1584, the mere prospect of such an anomaly as the King of France, 'the Eldest Son of the Church', being an excommunicated heretic meant civil war. The country had already been made desolate by seven 'Wars of Religion' in the past twenty-two years and now, unless there were some unexpected wisdom in high places, there would be an eighth.

King Henri's method of trying to prevent it had the merit of simplicity. He asked his brother-in-law of Navarre to visit Paris and go to Mass. He had no reason to suppose that the King of Navarre would refuse, for he had no strong religious convictions. He had been baptised a Catholic and, in his early years, until his Calvinist mother had gained sole control of him, he had been brought up in the orthodox faith. On the occasion of the Massacre of Saint Bartholomew when he was eighteen and a half he had returned to Catholicism to save his life and had practised it with every appearance of devotion until he had deemed it expedient for political reasons to renounce it.

The absence of religious convictions was accompanied by a temperament the reverse of puritanical, which made him the slave of woman after woman and provoked the sneers of the worldly-wise as well as the wrath of the godly. At thirty, Henry of Navarre seemed little but the replica of his father, Antony of Bourbon, first Prince of the Blood, whose popular nickname had been 'Caillette', the 'little quail', a bird noted for the change of colour of its coat and the habits which made it, since Biblical times, the symbol of lust.

Henri of France had thus every right to suppose that Henry of Navarre's response to his suggestion would be favourable. His letter exhorting him to 'come to Court and go to Mass because I desire to recognise you as my true heir and successor and to give you such rank and dignity near my person as the heir to the throne deserves' was carried by the Duc d'Épernon, himself a Gascon and *persona grata* with Navarre. The embassy was received with every mark of honour and Navarre pronounced himself deeply sensible of His Majesty's goodness in sending it. But, after careful thought, he refused. 'A man's religion,' he said, 'cannot be put on and off like his shirt.' In other matters he held himself entirely at His Majesty's orders and, even in this, he was prepared to obey if 'a free and universal council' adjudged it advisable.

His motives were shrewdly political. The assassination of William of Orange a month after 'Monsieur's' death had left European Protestantism without a leader. Navarre was the obvious candidate for such a position, which was a lucrative one, generously subsidised by Queen Elizabeth of England and carrying with it the acquisition of considerable territory in the Netherlands. At such a moment it would be foolish to abandon his present faith. Moreover, if he did so, he was likely to lose his own little kingdom of Béarn and his governorship of Guienne, because the Huguenots would certainly transfer their allegiance to his cousin, the gloomy, fanatical but trustworthy Calvinist, the Prince of Condé. The choice was thus not at all, as Épernon put it, 'between the Crown of France and a handful of psalms'. Henri III might have no crown to leave. Navarre was far from convinced that, when the inevitable civil war broke out, Henri would not be forced by the Duke of Guise to abdicate.

Henry, Duke of Guise, had been brought up in the family castle of Joinville by his grandmother, Antoinette de Bourbon, a formidable old lady who kept her coffin in the gallery connecting her apartments with the chapel that she might gaze on it as a *memento mori* as she went to her daily Mass. Her asceticism was such that on one occasion when her small grandson sought dutifully to kiss her she asked him: 'Why should you wish to embrace a handful of dry dust?'

Her eldest son, Francis, Duke of Guise, Henry's father, was one of the greatest soldiers of Europe; her second son, Charles Cardinal of Lorraine, was an outstanding statesman who happened also to be an able theologian and a dedicated ecclesiastic. Henry, when he was six, wrote to his father: 'I have heard some fine sermons from my uncle at Rheims, but I cannot repeat them to you for I assure you that they were so long that I cannot remember half that he said. He made me put on his robe and asked if I would not like to become a canon of Rheims, but I said I would rather be with you, breaking a lance or a sword to try the strength of my arm, for I would rather break lances than be shut up in an abbey in a monk's frock. I have been rather good lately.'

For the continuance of his education Henry was sent to Paris to attend the College of Navarre where the other two Henries—Henri de Valois, to become Henri III, King of France, and Henry of Bourbon, to become Henry, King of Navarre—were his school-fellows; but when he was nine his father returned from the wars (in which, among other victories, he had captured Calais from England) and henceforth he was the Duke's constant companion. The boy went everywhere with his father, following the course of events with a precocious, unchildlike attention.

Henry was ten weeks past his twelfth birthday when his idolised father was murdered by a Calvinist assassin inspired and paid by Gaspard de Coligny, Admiral of France, the leader of the Huguenots. The boy swore an oath of vengeance against Coligny and was taken back to Joinville where his uncle the Cardinal devoted his time and talents to preparing the young Duke for his destiny. As soon as he was sixteen, he obtained his grandmother's and his uncle's permission to join the Emperor in his crusade against the Turks. His father's death and his uncle's instruction had deepened Henry's religious feeling at the age when, in any case, it is apt to be most powerful and he wished to fight unequivocally for the Cross in the hardest of all schools.

Back in France, after campaigning in Hungary, he found an outlet for his newly-acquired military skill in the religious war that was raging by holding the ill-fortified town of Poitiers against Coligny's besieging force of 25,000 men,[1] for which exploit he gained the lyrical praise of French poets and a letter of gratitude from the Pope.

[1] See 'The Florentine Woman', p. 183, for details of the siege.

He was twenty-one when, having challenged Coligny to a duel and been refused, he was present at the Admiral's murder which was the first act of the massacre of Saint Bartholomew. To make it clear to everyone that his part in the holocaust was limited to fulfilling his filial vow of vengeance, he then saved the lives of a hundred Huguenots by giving them refuge in his Paris mansion, the Hôtel de Guise.

Three years later, attacking a force of German mercenaries whom the Huguenots had invited into France to aid their rebellion, Guise was badly wounded on the cheek. The wound left a scar not unlike that which his father had received in his wars and which had earned him the nickname of 'Le Balafré'. Now there was a second 'Balafré' and Paris went mad with enthusiasm over the symbolic succession. Like his father, Henry of Guise was the idol of the capital, which was always devotedly Catholic.

In his appearance he seemed one singled out by Nature for the rôle of popular hero. Six foot four in height and of such physical strength that he could swim upstream in armour; golden haired, blue-eyed with features of a delicate beauty; blessed with a temperament in which gloom and bitterness had no place and binding himself by a strict code of honour, he could, when he chose, exert irresistible charm. He spoke ill of no one and never refused a favour. With unfailing equanimity he bore the personal insults which King Henri, who loathed him for a variety of reasons, heaped on him.

But, as might have been predicted from his heredity, his upbringing and his experience of life, Henry of Guise had one great hatred—heresy. His passionate Catholicism alone would have ensured this, even without his observation of its disastrous effects on the country and the personal suffering he had

15

endured because of it. Consequently when in 1576 the Crown capitulated to the Huguenots by acknowledging Calvinism as an alternative religion for France, it was to him that the ordinary Catholics of France—the vast majority of the population—turned. The League of the Holy Trinity was formed, with him as its first Chief. It was, as the first article of its manifesto described it, an association of Catholic princes, lords and gentlemen for the restoration and upholding of the sole supremacy of the Catholic, Apostolic, Roman Church. It spread like lightning over the whole of France, though the King made desperate attempts to destroy it, first by proclaiming himself its Chief instead of Guise and then by ordering its suppression.

But, growing secretly, the League was now, eight years after its founding, stronger than ever and with the threat of a Calvinist heir to the throne it leapt into active life, winning support everywhere. For the prospect of a heretic king roused more than mere prejudice. The idea was repugnant to all the traditions of the French monarchy. St. Louis had laid it down in his *Perpetual Edict* that heresy caused a Prince of the Blood to forfeit all his rights and privileges and it was on descent from a younger son of St. Louis that the Bourbon claim rested. Now that Henry of Navarre had refused to return to the Catholic Church, the League was prepared to fight to block his succession. The insurrection would be formidable. The Leaguers controlled Champagne, Picardy, Burgundy, Berri, Dauphiné, Brittany and a considerable part of Normandy. Only in the south, in Guienne, Gascony and Languedoc, were they weak.

Guise, however, to whom loyalty was second nature, had no wish to lead a rebellion against the crown. The consequences of such an act would be incalculable. To escape from the impasse he turned to Henry of Navarre's uncle, the Cardinal of Bourbon.

Charles, Cardinal de Bourbon was a younger brother of Antony, the 'little quail' and no less vain, weak and voluptuous. He was now sixty-two but prematurely aged—'a wretched creature, decrepit and debauched, a gambler and a sot' as one of his critics somewhat over-vehemently described him. The Queen-Mother, Catherine de Medici, could, so the Spanish Ambassador reported, 'twist him round her little finger', adding: 'He is, however, a good Catholic.' But being a good Catholic merely meant, in his case, being a careful conformist and, above all, making himself agreeable to whatever Pope happened to occupy the Throne of St. Peter so that his comfortable life should not be interfered with.

He lived in considerable splendour at Gaillon in Normandy, about forty miles from Paris, in a princely château, which for the magnificence of its building and the beauty of its gardens, rivalled any royal residence. Though he had to fulfil occasional duties at Court, he spent most of his time at Gaillon, entirely governed by an intriguing and avaricious favourite domestic who, though his master had few secrets worth knowing, was very willing to sell them, such as they were.

Guise had thus no difficulty in acquainting himself with the Cardinal's affairs, his private life and his general habits in greater detail than his occasional meetings with him and their relationship—Guise's grandmother, Antoinette de Bourbon, was the Cardinal's aunt—had made possible, before he paid a visit to Gaillon to lay a proposition before him.

It was the Cardinal, Guise suggested, as the eldest representative of the Bourbons, not his nephew of Navarre, who was the real heir-presumptive to the Throne. In any case, Navarre had now barred himself and it was the Cardinal's duty both to Church and State to prepare himself to be King Charles X. He must petition the Pope to release him from his priestly vows in order that 'he might marry and bring up orthodox heirs to wear the Crown of St. Louis'. As a possible bride Guise suggested his own sister, the recently-widowed Duchess of Montpensier, whose wit, gaiety, energy and courage made her the 'Queen of the League'.

The Cardinal received the proposals with enthusiasm. He had, as a matter of fact, attempted to supplant his nephew twenty-two years ago when his brother, Antony, died. He had then solicited the Pope to release him from his vows and permit him to marry. His plea had been supported by the Papal Nuncio. But as the reason given was that 'the astrologers were predicting the speedy extinction of the House of Valois' the request was refused. Now, however, there were more cogent reasons and a refusal was not anticipated.

Henri III, hearing various rumours, decided to investigate for himself. When Épernon had returned with Navarre's refusal, the King announced his intention of visiting Gaillon. The step was deemed eccentric, but Henri had lately taken to perpetrating sudden surprises on the excuse *'ils me font connaître mon monde'*. There was a prevalent whisper that he was on the verge of madness. Only one man, his trusted friend and physician, Miron, knew that he had started the rumour himself.

Henri, at thirty-four—a few months older than Guise—precociously experienced in the ways of the world, satiated with pleasures, broken by the death of friends, disillusioned by the foolishness of wise statesmen, had manifested a passionate enthusiasm for the game of cup-and-ball which had just become the fashion in court circles. One day when he had insisted on practising for hours, Miron remarked: 'If Your Majesty continues much longer I shall think you are going mad.'

'Mad?'

'In a manner of speaking.'

'Not really mad?'

'You might say, sire, that all madness is a manner of speaking. Like beauty it can exist certainly only in the eye of the beholder.'

'And in your eyes I appear mad?'

'No. But you will if you continue longer in such a lunatic occupation.'

Henri paused in the occupation, considered for a minute or two and then said: 'My dear friend, you will let it discreetly be known about court—in whispers, not in shouts—that you fear I am going mad.'

'But, Your Majesty, I didn't say—'

'Of course you didn't. But you have given me an idea. A madman has liberty. He is allowed to do and say what others are not. He can understand men's minds because they do not hide their thoughts from him, thinking he cannot understand. It will be easier for me to rule if people think I am mad. Thank you, my dear Miron.'

The rumour had even reached the Cardinal who received the King with a mixture of great deference and anxious concern. One day when they were walking in one of the pleasaunces for which the gardens of the château were famous, the King suddenly said: 'Will you answer me a question?'

'Certainly, if I can.'

'As you know, everything in this world is uncertain. Supposing I should die today, the crown would fall in direct line to your house. Should that happen, would it go to you or to your nephew?'

'I pray God to call me from the world before such a calamity happens. I shall be dead long before you, sire.'

'But if you are not?'

'I have never given a thought to a thing so unlikely and contrary to the order of nature.'

'Yes, yes. But how often is the order of nature changed as God pleases! What I want to know is, if such an introversion should occur, would you or would you not dispute the succession with your nephew?'

The Cardinal tried to evade a direct reply, but the King, with a malicious pleasure, persisted in pressing him. At last he said: 'As Your Majesty commands me to tell you, although the possibility of such an event has never crossed my mind, yet if such a disaster as your death should occur, I will not deny that, as the crown would belong to me and not to my nephew, I should firmly resolve not to give it up to him.'

The King laughed and patting the Cardinal condescendingly on the shoulder said: 'Va, mon bon ami, le Châtelet vous donnerait la couronne, mais la Cour vous l'ôterait.'[2]

The Cardinal was now certain that Henri was not always in his right mind.

Henry of Navarre, when rumours reached him of his uncle's intentions, wrote light-heartedly: 'They tell me, dear uncle, that some people want to make you King. Bid them make you Pope. It would suit you much better and, besides,

[2] This somewhat obscure *bon mot* of Henri, which is hardly translatable, meant that the crown might possibly be given to the cardinal by the Châtelet —i.e. the rogues and vagabonds of Paris—but that the nobles and great officers of the realm would soon force him to abdicate.

you would then be greater than them all.' The Cardinal was not amused.

Henry's own Huguenot subjects were not insensitive to the changed status of their sovereign and his Calvinist mentor, the stern Duplessis-Mornay, told him bluntly: 'These amours to which you give so much time and which have hitherto been so public, are no longer suitable or possible. It is now time that you should make love to the whole of Christendom and especially to France.' Henry laughed and did the next best thing. He fell genuinely in love for the first time.

It was a curious romance. After a bewildering series of mistresses of every age and station, the last being La Fosseuse, a girl of fifteen who had borne him a child, he suddenly noticed a woman he had known since boyhood, the Countess of Gramont, 'la Belle Corisande'.

She was thirty—only a few months younger than himself—and since childhood had been the close friend of his sister Catherine who, in the absence of his wife, presided over his court. In spite of her *sobriquet* Corisande was not particularly beautiful though, in addition to fair hair, blue eyes and a skin of notable whiteness, she had that incipient double-chin which was the age's *sine qua non* for feminine attractiveness. She was a Catholic and, in that bastion of Calvinism, she insisted on going to Mass publicly with her co-religionists, a motley handful which, Henry teased her, consisted of 'the little Lambert girl, a Moor, a Basque in a green robe, a magician named Bertrand, an English page, a jester and a footman'.

Corisande's charm lay in her gaiety, her courage and her loyalty (she was the only one of Henry's numerous mistresses who was faithful to him) and, matching his own temperament, a worldly-wisdom which led her to annotate his letters with cynical marginal comments when he indulged in such well-worn phrases as: 'Believe my fidelity to be pure and un-spotted. I have always remained fixed in the fidelity and service I have vowed to you, as God is my witness.'

The letters she preferred were those connected with shared simplicities such as any husband might write to any wife, like that which he sent her when he was on a journey inspecting some of the towns in his kingdom: 'How I wish you were here. It is of all the places I have ever seen the one most after your own heart. It is an island surrounded by wooded marshlands, where at every hundred paces one comes upon canals which wood-cutters use to transport their timber in boats. The water is clean and flows slowly. The canals are of every width, the boats of all sizes. A thousand gardens lie among the wilderness, all to be reached by water alone. The river flows by the foot of the castle which is as habitable as that at Pau. There are many kinds of singing birds and sea-fowl. I send you some of their feathers. One might live here pleasantly in peace and safely in war, rejoicing with one's love or lamenting her in absence.'

Henry was not disposed to disturb the new dimension of love he had found either by himself going to Paris or by welcoming his wife home from her sojourn there.

2

The Misadventures of Margot

Marguerite de Valois, wife of Henry of Navarre, sister of Henri III, was now thirty-two and her celebrated beauty was a trifle overblown. If it was still true that, as one visitor had put it, 'who has not seen Margot has seen neither France nor the court' the reasons had slightly changed. She was still a superb figure, a cynosure for all eyes. She could still converse for hours with scholars in Italian, Spanish, Greek and Latin. She could still control a political situation or conduct a court intrigue with more brilliance and pertinacity than anyone else in France, even her mother, Catherine de Medici. And she could still charm anyone she wanted into bed—a power she used so often and so openly that her exercise of it had become the dominant factor in her reputation.

A deeply religious woman, she was too wise to confuse religion with morality and might well, as far as her amorous adventures went, have anticipated the remark: 'Dieu me pardonnera; c'est Son métier.' But in matters of faith she was unsparing. 'What helped me on the road of devotion,' she wrote in her *Memoirs*, 'was reading in the fair and universal book of Nature so many marvels concerning its Creator. They are surely such that every intelligent soul, making his knowledge a ladder of which God is the last and highest step, stands there rapt in adoration of this wonderful light. And, making a perfect circle, the spirit finds its only pleasure in following that Chain which, proceeding from God Himself, returns to God Himself, the Originator and the End of all things. And sorrow (in contradistinction to joy which whirls away from us the consciousness of our actions) awakes our soul in its inmost self which, gathering all its forces to reject evil and to seek out good, thinks and re-thinks without ceasing how it may choose the sovereign good, in order to bring it to the state of tranquillity which best inclines us to come to the knowledge and love of God.'

Her Deism was, in practice, sharpened and defined by her acceptance of the Church. Even as a girl when, for a short time, Huguenotism had been a fashionable fad at court and she had been told that 'only stupid people are Catholics', she had faced beatings rather than agree. At nineteen, she had resisted as far as she was able her forced marriage to Henry of Navarre and, when at last she yielded to the commands of the family, it was on the understanding that she could continue to practise her own religion. 'I have been brought up in the Catholic Faith,' she said, 'and I will not abandon it for the greatest monarch in the world.'

The marriage was the disaster of her life. Not only were she and Henry completely incompatible sexually, but there was a continual social tension of which one expression was her preference for two baths a day and his reluctant acceptance of one bath a year. Eventually they arrived at a *modus vivendi* based on an identity of political interest and a polite tolerance of each other's *affaires*. But, when possible, they preferred to live apart. She was out of her element away from the French court

and her one enforced visit to Nérac as Queen of Navarre inspired the comment: 'One lives here without the slightest
novelty. Always the same preoccupations, always the same
bêtises. Gascony is so boring that it can only produce news
exactly like itself.'

But her marriage was more tragic in what it prevented than
in what it provoked. It prevented her marrying her first—
and, in one sense, her only—love, the Duke of Guise. In her
fashion, she remained faithful to him and she was at the
moment not only supporting the League and using her *salon*
in Paris in its interests but was actually attempting the para-
doxical impossibility of inducing her husband to join it.

The most disturbing element in Margot's life was, however,
neither Henry of Navarre nor Henry of Guise but her brother,
Henri III. When she was seventeen and he eighteen, their
mutual attraction had become so strong that they became
virtually a secret society of two, bound exclusively to each
other by their birth, their half-Italian family background, their
tastes, their intelligence, their sense of humour, their dislike
of the banal and their impatience of convention. Margot worshipped: Henri allowed himself to be worshipped. If he
recommended a new book to her, she would read it straight
through, oblivious of food and sleep. When they amused
themselves with a battle of wits, the Court would fall silent
to listen to them, 'for whether in seriousness or gaiety, nothing
was more entrancing than to hear those two talk as they
wished'. When they danced, the brother leading the sister
in a *pavane*, 'one body, one soul, one will' the other dancers
would leave the floor, 'all eyes on them, ravished by the lovely
sight'.

By the nature of things, the idyll could not last, but its consequences shaped the rest of their lives. The Court assumed

incest and Henri's and Margot's maniacal jealousy of each other went far to confirm the suspicion. It became the mainspring of their actions as each tried to destroy the other, playing a deadly game as private to themselves and as elegantly as their early contests of wit.

The origin of the hatred was Henri's discovery of Margot's love for Guise and his thwarting of it by forcing Guise's immediate marriage to someone else. ('If you so much as look at my sister again,' he told him, 'you will get a knife between your ribs.') Her reply was, when a suitable occasion presented itself, to have Henri's two most beloved *mignoss* killed, one by hired assassins, the other in a murderous duel arranged by Guise. She plotted continuously with her younger brother, 'Monsieur', to dethrone Henri and now that 'Monsieur' was dead she was pinning her hopes in that respect on Guise and the League.

At the moment, Margot was on the defensive. She was aware that plans were afoot to get the Pope to annul her marriage. Philip of Spain was a widower for the fourth time and of all his wives he had loved most dearly his second, Margot's elder sister, Elisabeth of Valois. He was now suggesting that, if Navarre and Margot were free of each other, he should marry Margot and Navarre should marry her niece, one of the Infantas, Elisabeth's daughter. Whether Henri knew of this and, if so, what his attitude was to it, or whether he had plans of his own for her future, Margot did not know but she was apprehensive of the real purpose of the visit to the Vatican of the twenty-two-year-old Duc de Joyeuse, who shared with the older Duc d'Épernon the official Royal affection. The ostensible reason was the fulfilment of a vow Henri had made to visit the shrine of Notre Dame de Loretto to intercede for a son and an inquiry as to whether the construction of a new chapel in the church at Loretto would be considered a sufficient substitute for a personal visit. But no one, least of all Margot, supposed that this explanation had any purpose but to deceive the gullible and she determined at all costs to find out what lay behind it.

As she was not living in her apartments at the Louvre but in her Hôtel de la Couture-Sainte-Catherine, she found it more difficult to procure reliable information. Her lover of the moment, Jacques de Harlay, Marquis de Chanvallon, was reputedly the most beautiful young man in France. She was moved to write of him, 'son beau tout, seul soleil de son âme, sa vie, beau miracle de la nature, ses beaux yeux, seuls soleils de mon âme par eux, tout feu, toute flamme' ... But he was not very intelligent and quite useless in a matter of delicate diplomatic espionage and she was forced to employ more direct means to gratify her curiosity. She hired four bravoes to intercept the royal courier who took Henri's letters to Joyeuse—usually two large sheets written in the King's own hand. The masked hirelings attacked the messenger, wounding him dangerously, on the road from Paris, abstracted the necessary packet and brought the documents to Margot.

She read them with growing disappointment and anger. They contained no hint of the weighty matters she wished to know. They were witty and scurrilous accounts of happenings at court, including most of the gossip she knew and adding, for good measure, a considerable amount about herself, much of it inaccurate. Henri suggested, for example, that she used her bevy of flaxen-haired pages for other purposes than cutting a little of their hair each day for the making of her flaxen wigs. And there were remarks about Chanvallon which even his bitterest enemy would have hesitated to make.

Margot's rage, however, was nothing to Henri's when he

27

heard about the attack on his courier. Without any evidence, he ascribed it immediately to her. He was on the way to join his wife, Queen Louise, at Bourbon, where she was taking the baths, but he ordered his coach to turn about and make immediately for Paris. Margot was presiding over a court ball at the Louvre, in the absence of the two Queens, Louise and the Queen-Mother, Catherine. At the height of the festivity, when all the rooms were crowded with guests, the King stormed into the ball-room and went straight to the daïs on which Margot was enthroned. In the silence caused by his sudden and unexpected entry, he recapitulated in clear tones a catalogue of what he called her 'sycophants and lovers', beginning with Guise and ending with Chanvallon. He also accused her of aborting her child by Chanvallon and ended his tirade with a command to leave Paris within twenty-four hours: 'Go back to your husband: you are polluting the air here.'

Margot listened with unruffled composure and with some interest. He was quite wrong about the supposed abortion. Chanvallon's child had been born—a son who was now safely with a fostermother.[1] Also Henri had omitted at least three of her lovers as well as including two of her pages who had never given her anything but their hair. Henri was obviously not as well-informed as he should have been.

She waited until he had finished, said no word in reply, rose with a dignity which none but she could have assumed, made a profound reverence and unhurriedly left the room, accompanied by Chanvallon and her ladies. Back at her Hôtel, she said an immediate farewell to her lover whom she implored to ride without stopping until he had crossed the fron-

---

[1] According to tradition, he became a monk and was known as Frère Ange.

tier. She then spent what was left of the night in writing letters to the principal Leaguers who had witnessed the scene, denying all the King's charges and hoping that 'such a contradiction as this is more suitable to my royal station than to have publicly retorted to the abusive epithets of my brother and king'.

In the morning, Henri sent another message ordering her to leave Paris before nightfall 'as Her Majesty would be more suitably placed under the protection of her husband, the King of Navarre, for at the court of France her presence was conducive of more evil than good'. He also ordered the arrest of Chanvallon, unaware that the young man was already beyond his jurisdiction.

Margot left the capital immediately and broke her journey to dine at Bourg-la-Reine. An hour after her departure Henri set out on the same road and passed through Bourg-la-Reine without taking any notice of her. But as she went on her way to the village of Palaiseau where she intended to spend the night, she was stopped by Larchant, the Captain of the King's Guard, with a force of sixty archers. Larchant presented her with an order for arrest, signed by Henri. She was turned out of her litter while it was searched and every article and paper in it seized for the King's inspection. Her ladies had their *tourets-de-nez* torn from their faces and their clothes searched immodestly by the archers for documents they were supposed to be carrying. The Queen's two principal ladies-in-waiting, Madame de Duras and Mademoiselle de Bêthune, were arrested and sent to the Bastille on the charge of procuring abortions. Her physician, her diplomatic secretary, her equerry and her first gentleman-usher were also arrested and taken to the King for examination. When, guarded by the archers, the company reached Palaiseau, Larchant, with half a dozen of the guard, forced his way into Margot's room at midnight, ordered her to get up while they searched the bed, rifled her coffers but found no trace of the letters stolen from the courier or indeed any document of any sort which might justify Henri's conduct. When he received news of this he reflected that Margot, when she set her mind to it, had always managed to out-manoeuvre him. He had not a shred of proof of what he was certain she had done.

The Imperial Ambassador (who had already informed his master 'You would not believe the things that go on at the French Court') wrote: 'The King, now his rage is over, already repents of having branded his own blood with infamy. All persons acquainted with the character of the Queen of Navarre predict that she will soon find ample expedients to avenge the flagrant insults she has suffered.'

Margot wrote to the Pope, to Guise and to her mother asking their help and advice, while to her husband she sent a letter, protesting her innocence of the charges and demanding that he take suitable steps against Henri on her behalf.

Henri, however, had written first to Navarre—a flippant relation of 'the adventures which had recently happened to the Queen his wife' and commanded him to receive her.

The last thing Henry of Navarre wanted, involved as he was with Corisande, was the presence of Margot. It was not that he was ignorant of Margot's misdemeanours, still less that he was surprised or shocked by them. He merely did not want her in Nérac lest, in the absence of anything else to occupy her mind, she should make mischief with Corisande. Accordingly he wrote to her, forbidding her to return to him until she had vindicated her honour. He also sent Duplessis-

Mornay to Lyons, where King Henri now was, to demand an explanation of the royal actions.

'The King of Navarre,' said Duplessis-Mornay, 'demands, sire, that if his consort and Your Majesty's sister be in fact guilty of the crimes of which you have accused her you will punish her; and if, on the contrary, she has been calumniated you will punish her slanderers.'

Henri replied that he had been misled by false reports and that, as soon as the Queen of Navarre was back in Nérac, the whole matter would be closed and forgotten.

'But, sire,' objected the dour precisian, 'what will the princes of Christendom say if my master receives back his wife without any explanation after Your Majesty's charges?'

'Say?' said Henri angrily, 'Say? They will say that the King of Navarre has received back the sister of his King and that there was nothing else he could do!'

Duplessis-Mornay answered that his master had decided not to receive back his wife until her reputation was cleared.

Henri lost his temper. 'Go back to the King your master as you call him and tell him that, if he takes such a course, I will place such a yoke on his neck as would bend the back of a potentate as mighty as the Grand Seignior. Go and tell him so. Get out of my court! Your master is fittingly served by such a paltry servant as you.'

On reflection, however, the King thought it best to write a letter to his brother-in-law rather than to leave matters to Duplessis-Mornay's reporting. 'Kings, mon frère,' he wrote, withdrawing the charges, 'have before this committed errors; and the most virtuous princesses have not been exempt from foul slanders, in witness of which remember all the libels current respecting that most estimable personage, the late Queen of Navarre, your mother.'

When Navarre received the letter, he roared: 'First he tells me I'm *cocu* and now he implies I'm the son of a bitch.'

But he allowed Margot to come back.

3

The Dilemma of the Duke of Guise

The Duke of Guise was in a dilemma. As far as France was concerned his duty, as he saw it, was simple. He was the Catholic champion on whose loyalty the King could rely to resist the forces of heresy endeavouring to subvert the monarchy. The League, representing the great majority of Frenchmen, was the bulwark of the throne. To emphasise this and to make it clear to everyone that he had no personal ambition, in spite of *canards* that he himself was aiming at the Crown, he had insisted on the Cardinal de Bourbon as the heir-presumptive so that the succession should remain legitimately with the Bourbon Princes of the Blood. Had Henry of Navarre, for whom Guise had no personal dislike, returned to Catholicism, he would have been quite prepared to support him.

The issue, however, was not so simple. The religious question had split Europe and home politics were bedevilled by international alignments. England and the Netherlands and the German mercenaries of John Casimir[1] were ranged on

[1] See *The Last of the Valois*, p. 137

the side of the Huguenots. Philip of Spain, whose nephew the Duke of Parma was successfully reducing the revolted Spanish Netherlands to obedience, was as devoted a Catholic as Guise and was being forced into the position of the Catholic champion of Europe.

But the European situation, in general so much wider in its issues than the French, was for Guise narrower. It had shrunk to a family matter, for the pivot of it was his cousin, Mary Queen of Scots, who, when he was seven, had become Queen of France. He remembered vividly how she had come to Joinville when he was nine and she nineteen to say farewell to Antoinette, her grandmother and his. He had never forgotten her beauty and her wit and, above all, her understanding in treating his boyishness, though she was a widowed Queen, on terms of equality. He did not forget, either, their grandmother's attempts to persuade her to remain in France as Duchess of Touraine until another suitable husband was found for her and, when Antoinette realised that her granddaughter was determined to go to Scotland come what might, the old lady's impatient: 'You're a fool, Mary, to adventure yourself among barbarians when there's no need. You will rue it.'

Mary had rued it indeed. Dethroned by her Calvinist subjects led by her bastard brother, Moray (who had always 'looked sideways through his fingers' at the Crown and eventually gained the Regency) she had fled to England. But Elizabeth of England refused to meet her[2] and Mary had spent sixteen years in captivity, surrounded by spies and *agents-provocateurs*, as well as apparently faithful servants

---

[2] As certain so-called 'historical plays', in particular Schiller's, make great drama of their meeting, it may be as well to remind the reader that, in spite of all Mary's pleas and Elizabeth's promises, they never met.

who had in fact been 'planted' on her by her enemies, in an attempt to get her to make some move against Elizabeth which would justify the English Queen in killing her.

Mary was, in the eyes of every Catholic in Europe from the Pope downwards, the legitimate Queen of England and her rescue had become the main object of Catholic strategy. Don John of Austria, when his half-brother, King Philip of Spain, had appointed him Governor of the Netherlands, had epitomised the matter in a letter: 'The true remedy for the evil condition of the Netherlands is that England should be in the power of a person devoted and well-affected to Your Majesty's service and it is my opinion that the ruin of these countries will result from the contrary position in English affairs. At Rome and elsewhere the rumour prevails that Your Majesty and His Holiness have thought of me as the best instrument you could choose to carry out your designs, indignant as you both are by the evil proceedings of the Queen of England and the wrongs she has done to the Queen of Scots, especially in sustaining heresy.'

In other words, Don John, with the approval of the Pope and Philip of Spain, was to marry Mary Queen of Scots, when he had liberated her with the aid of Spanish troops and set her on the English throne.

Don John, on his way to take up his post in the Netherlands, had paid a secret visit to Joinville to consult Guise on the best way of accomplishing the liberation. A cypher for correspondence between Joinville and Madrid had been arranged and it had been established that, in this foreign enterprise, Philip of Spain and Henry of Guise should act together. But it was specifically excluded that Spanish troops should ever be used in France or against French interests.

When Don John died the understanding between Philip

and Guise continued. Though the King was prodigal of promises and protestations of affection, he remained true to his
maxim 'In matters of consequence it is best to walk on leaden
feet' and took no practical steps. It was left to Guise to com-
mission an English agent to make an inventory of the English
ports, to inquire into the amount of provisions that might be
obtained on landing, to discover how many horses could be
easily procured for the transport of artillery and to assure
English Catholics that as soon as Mary Queen of Scots was
released and on the throne all foreigners would leave the
country. Guise pledged himself to drive them out, if necessary,
by force.

The Duke was right to realise how intensely the English
disliked foreign interference and Philip, who had had practical
experience of it during his five years as King of England,
recognised it even more vividly. Yet, because of their own
dedicated Catholicism, which put the Faith above every other
consideration, both consistently misread the English situation
and failed to take into account that there was a marked disposition among Catholics in England to repel any invader
and a firm aversion to organising any revolt.[3]

And the Queen of Scots herself had written at this moment
to her ambassador in Paris: 'I charge you to make it known
to my relations and friends over there that I beg them to desist
from all practises and negotiations, if they have any in hand,
that tend to the disturbance of this state, the welfare of which,
its peace and preservation, I place before any satisfaction and
advantage for myself.'

Yet, whatever anyone might say, the religious struggle had

[3] Every scrap of evidence we possess, without exception, demonstrates the
falsity of Dr. Conyers Read's remark (in his *Mr. Secretary Walsingham*) that
English Catholics were ready 'to rise in support of any invader who came
against Elizabeth in the name of their faith'.

now transferred itself to the international arena and Guise's comfortable theory of support for the King at home combined with action for the Faith abroad, was rapidly becoming untenable in practice.

King Henri himself was largely to blame for it, by making his own Catholicism suspect. When representatives of the Netherlands arrived in France to offer him the sovereignty of the Low Countries if he would declare war on Spain on their behalf, offering him twelve towns in Flanders as a guarantee of good faith and a monthly sum of 100,000 crowns towards the expenses of the war, he received them graciously and, despite Catholic protests, announced: 'I do not regard the Flemings as rebels, but as an oppressed people: and France has always been the champion of the unfortunate.'

A week later a special English embassy arrived, ostensibly to bring him the Order of the Garter, which Queen Elizabeth had bestowed on him, actually to urge him to accept the Flemish proposal and offer him 1,000 cavalry, 5,000 infantry and a third of the expenses of the war if he did. Henri was invested with the Collar of the Order of the Garter in the Church of the Augustinians, where two great pictures of his founding of his own Order of Saint-Esprit adorned the walls. Members of that Order were present, as well as the delegations from Flanders and England; and the Parisians, though unaware of the secret diplomacy behind it all, saw in the King's acceptance of the Garter and the excessive pomp which surrounded the ceremonies, a sign of his inclination towards heresy.

On the face of it, no accusation could be more absurd. Henri, in his religious devotions, his founding of orders of monks, his membership of the Flagellants and his pilgrimages through Paris scourging himself, his liberal benefactions to church after church, might seem the devoutest of the devout. Yet there was a neurotic overstrain about it which did not recommend it to the simple Parisians and the discovery that, in the King's private chapel at Vincennes, the candlesticks on the altar were in the form of satyrs and the gold paten was engraved with a scene from the *Iliad* depicting the love of Achilles and Patroclus did nothing to reassure them.

From the pulpits of Paris, Henri was accused of atheism, tyranny and sodomy, while the Duke of Guise and the Cardinal de Bourbon were extolled as 'holy and acceptable to the Lord, the chosen, the defenders of the Faith and the hope of benighted France'. At St. Severin, the famous *curé*, Jean Prévost, who had set up in his churchyard an enormous painting of the tortures which had been recently inflicted in London on the Catholic martyrs, Edmund Campion and his companions, as an object lesson in what might be expected in Paris under a heretic king, made abusive orations against Queen Elizabeth and Henry of Navarre. In many of the churches the double cross of Jerusalem, the symbol of the Lorraine princes, was set up on the altars. It was said to be fitting that the Guises, because of their double portion of Christian zeal, should have such an emblem and it soon became the crest of the League.[4]

In order to protect the King's person, Épernon persuaded Henri to dismiss the majority of the gentlemen of his household, who were mainly members of great houses associated with either the Huguenots or the League, and to replace them with a special guard composed exclusively of his own nomi-

[4] Huguenots naturally had another interpretation:
  Mais, dites-moi, que signifie
  Que les ligueurs ont double-croix?
  C'est qu'en La Ligue on crucifie
  Jésus-Christ encore une fois.

nees, mostly Gascons like himself. There were forty-five of them—a number which, as the favourite explained, was based on the utilitarian properties of the number three.

'Three,' said Épernon, 'is not only the divine number; it is the most convenient on earth. As we know that God is Trinity in Unity, so I would hold—though I am no theologian, as you are, sire—that on earth the perfect Unity is a Trinity.'

'Can you make that clearer?' said the King.

'Let us take a simple thing like a horse. If a man owns three horses, he is provided against ever having to walk. When the first has to be rested, there is the second at hand; and, in case of an accident or disease, the second can be replaced by the third. Thus, to have effectively one horse, one must have three horses.'

'You could make it any number,' said Henri, 'but I will not dispute it till I see where you are leading.'

'I am trying to show you that forty-five is the perfect number for your guard. You will always have three times fifteen gentlemen—fifteen in service, thirty resting. Each day you will have fifteen, rested and active, by your side—Five on your right hand, five on your left, two in front and three behind. With them you can move freely where you will, even among the mobs in the streets, for no one will dare attack you with such a guard.'

The *Quarante-cinq* was thus duly installed in the Louvre in that December of 1584. It consisted exclusively of unmarried men, for the most part 'cadets and without the means of maintaining a great appearance'. They entered into an engagement for two years and three months and their pay was 1,200 crowns a year. All their expenses were borne by the King to whom they were bound by a personal and particular oath to render him without question any service whatever he should require of them. Their captain was—under Épernon—François de Montpézat, Baron de Laugnac, an unscrupulous bravo, famous for his murderous cruelty. From the outset they were hated by the Parisians, who called them the *coup-jarrets*—cut-throats —and compared them unfavourably even with the detested *mignons* of earlier years. The *mignons* at least had elegance, *panache* and breeding as well as a fantastic physical courage. The *Quarante-cinq* were merely vulgar murderers, well represented by Laugnac who, it was not forgotten, in a recent duel had not only struck his adversary several blows after he had fallen but had watched his death-agonies with a cold cruelty which had revolted even his friends. Yet, had the Parisians known it, it was for precisely these qualities that the Forty Five had been chosen and bound to the King by special oath. Henri had now to his hand a perfect instrument for political assassination.

On the last day of the year, his thirty-fourth birthday, Henry of Guise held a secret conference at Joinville in which at last he faced the facts of the situation and resolved his dilemma of conflicting loyalties, by acknowledging the paramouncy of the religious issue and admitting it was indivisible throughout Europe.

He had called to the conference his two younger brothers, Charles, Duke of Mayenne, who was thirty and Louis, Cardinal of Guise, who was twenty-nine. Mayenne had a barrel-like corpulence (Margot described him as 'quite deformed by fatness') and huge hands 'round as legs of mutton'. He wore a square beard, which accentuated his size less than the fashionable pointed one. Both in appearance and personality he conspicuously lacked the charm of his elder brother. He was dry, phlegmatic and practical; economical to the point of meanness where Henry was lavishly over-generous; a cautious, slow-moving soldier where Henry was gallantly reckless. Mayenne was no leader of men, still less an inspirer of them, as Henry was, but his loyalty to his brother was absolute. His reliable qualities had been apparent from his early boyhood and, though he was only nine when his father had been murdered, the great Duke had prophesied that Charles would eventually be 'the stay of the family'.

Louis, the youngest brother, had been Archbishop of Rheims since he was nineteen and Cardinal of Guise since he was twenty-three and his ecclesiastical duties, however nominal, had inculcated a certain gravity which tempered his energetic enthusiasms. In a sense he mirrored both his brothers, combining the *panache* of Henry with the caution of Charles.

Other members of the family who were invited to the Joinville conference were the Dukes of Aumale and Elboeuf, uncles of the three brothers, the Duke of Nemours, Guise's step-father, and the Duke of Mercoeur, their Lorraine cousin, who, although Queen Louise's brother, was in sympathy with the League. None of them attended in person—Nemours because he was too crippled with gout to move—but they were all prepared to accept Guise's decisions.

François de Roucherolles, Sieur de Mayneville, who was Guise's principal agent with the League in Paris, was empowered by the Cardinal de Bourbon to act on his behalf and King Philip of Spain was represented by his ambassador, the formidable Bernadino de Mendoza who had just been transferred from London to Paris.

The terms of this religious alliance between Lorraine, Spain and the League were speedily formulated. The French engaged themselves to ensure that Catholicism was the only permitted religion in France and to pursue '*à outrance* and until they had annihilated them' the heretics who refused to return to the Church. The decrees of the Council of Trent were to be proclaimed and accepted in their entirety.[5] Heresy was to be similarly fought in the Netherlands. The King of Spain, on his side, agreed to provide a subsidy of 600,000 crowns in the first six months of the outbreak of any hostilities in which the League might become involved and an additional 50,000 crowns a month as long as those hostilities lasted. All such sums were to be refunded by the Cardinal de Bourbon when he became Charles X. The Cardinal also promised the cession of Béarn and Lower Navarre to Spain. The Pact of Joinville was to be kept secret and the parties bound themselves not to treat separately with any ruler whatsoever. The Union was to be a single sword forged to defend the Catholic Faith wherever it was attacked. Guise's dilemma was resolved at last.

[5] The Tridentine decrees were accepted as the definition of the Catholic faith from their promulgation in 1563 until 1968 when Pope Paul VI composed and enacted a new Mass contravening their essential theology.

4

The King and his Favourites

The day after the meeting at Joinville, New Year's Day, 1585, King Henri issued an edict over which he had laboured for some time. It revised the etiquette of the Royal Household, and in voluminous detail prescribed propriety for even the most trivial actions. It prohibited certain oaths. It forbade the appointment of successors in any office, however humble, because 'it serves to excite an unChristian desire for the demise of the present occupier'. It devoted two long sections to the ceremonies to be observed in presenting a glass of cold water to the King on awaking in the morning. It reduced the number of Privy Councillors and enacted that in winter they were to attend the Council in robes of violet velvet but that in summer satin was to be substituted. This clause particularly irritated the more impecunious nobles who grudged the expense entailed by the alteration of their official dress. But the item which caused an explosion of indignation from everyone was the clause enacting that the King's two favourites, the Duc d'Épernon and the Duc de Joyeuse, should take precedence of everyone but the Princes of the Blood. In one sense, however, it was logical enough, because the King was in the habit of referring to them as his eldest sons, though most people doubted whether his relationship with them could with any accuracy be described as paternal.

Épernon was thirty, a bold, unscrupulous Gascon with all the Gascon arrogance and wit. He was born Nogaret de la Valette, the second son of an official concerned with provisioning the army. Joyeuse—Anne d'Arques, eldest son of Marshal de Joyeuse, of old and distinguished lineage—was twenty-three, gallant, honourable and more sincerely devoted to Henri as a man than anyone since the dead Quélus. As far as was possible, he took something of Quélus's place in the King's heart.

An essential difference between the favourites was that whereas Épernon retained much of his hold on Henri by his witty and scurrilous recitals of the doings of some of the courtiers and his readiness to play embarrassing tricks on them, Joyeuse was prepared to perpetrate practical jokes on the King. The most notorious of these was the affair of the *Sarbacane*, in which he joined forces with one of the surviving *mignons*, Saint-Luc, and with the irrepressible Duchesse de Montpensier to frighten the King into cleansing the Court. The Duchess provided a brass tube which Saint-Luc, whose room was next to the King's, introduced, by perforating the wooden partition, into the alcove close to the royal bed. Accordingly one night Henri was roused from sleep by Joyeuse's disguised voice close to his ear whispering denunciations and admonitions. At first the King paid little heed, imagining that he had been dreaming, and composed himself to sleep again. But the hissing whisper continued and Henri, thinking himself addressed by an angelic messenger of Divine wrath, leapt out of bed and remained on his knees till dawn.

Inevitably the trick was discovered and Saint-Luc, warned in time by the Duke of Guise, fled the capital. But Joyeuse was forgiven, much to Épernon's surprise and annoyance, by the infatuated King.

Joyeuse, devoutly Catholic, was always on good terms with Guise, whereas Épernon inclined towards the Huguenots. Henri's recognition of this was betokened by his sending Épernon on the embassy to Navarre and Joyeuse on the mission to the Pope. The two favourites were, however, bound to each other by the marriage of Joyeuse's brother to Épernon's sister, the eighteen-year-old Catherine de la Valette, whom the King described as 'the greatest saint in my dominions'. The girl, needing no angelic visitation to convince her of the degradation and impiety of the Court, was so appalled by her observation of it that she devoted her life to making some reparation. She gave away a fortune to the poor and, not content with such—as she considered it—easy charity, she devoted days and nights to nursing the poor and friendless in the hospitals of Paris. One of the few occasions when Henri was at one with the Parisians was when he spontaneously knelt, as sometimes he did, to kiss the hem of her dress.

The King had determined to attach the favourites to the Royal House by marrying them to the Queen's two younger sisters, Margaret and Christine of Lorraine. Though Christtine, destined for Épernon, was not yet of marriageable age, the wedding of Joyeuse and Margaret in the September of 1582 had been a memorable occasion. So that there might be no legitimate cause for jealousy between the Dukes, the King had paid in advance the same marriage portion—400,000 gold crowns, the dowry of a Daughter of France—to Épernon on the day that Joyeuse received Margaret's and he had also conferred on Épernon places and pensions of equal value to Joyeuse's new estate of Limours. Joyeuse had been appointed Admiral of France, Épernon Colonel-General of Infantry and Governor of Saintonge and Touraine.

The wedding itself and the subsequent festivities had exceeded in splendour anything in Henri's reign, not excluding the installation of the Knights of the Order of *Saint-Esprit*. The Tuscan Ambassador put the cost at 'more than two millions in gold'. The King and Joyeuse were dressed exactly alike, 'their doublets and vests being so covered with embroidery and precious stones', recorded a diarist, 'that it was impossible to calculate their value. The making-up of them alone cost 10,000 crowns. Seventeen fêtes were given by the King and the nobility related to the newly-married couple and at all these masquerades, jousts, dances, etc., the guests were forbidden to appear twice in the same attire and even the jewels of the ladies had to be worn each time in different devices'.

Of the seventeen marriage festivals, that given by the Cardinal de Bourbon had been intended to be the most magnificent as well as the most original. An aquatic procession had been arranged to take place on the Seine and an enormous barge in the form of a triumphal car had been constructed to convey the King, the Queen, the princes and princesses, down the river to the Pré-aux-Clercs. The car was to have been drawn by small boats disguised as sea-horses, led by tritons, accompanied by sirens, with twenty-four whales, dolphins and other sea-beasts disporting themselves alongside. Inside the various creatures were concealed bands of musicians with trumpets, violins and hautbois. Unfortunately nothing had been able to induce this wonderful machine, intended to astonish as well as to please the king, to get under way and after having waited two hours while the workmen wrestled with it in vain, Henri, remarking that he perceived 'que c'étaient des bêtes qui commandaient d'autres bêtes' had got into his coach and driven to the Cardinal's residence.

Apart from this, however, the festivities had been in every sense of the term a spectacular success, even though 'everybody was amazed at so great luxury and such an enormous and superfluous expense at a time which was not one of the best in the world but very hard and severe for the people eaten and gnawed to the bone, by soldiers in the country and by new taxes in the capital'. The Chancellor had actually remonstrated with the King, only to be met with: 'Now I have got my sons off my hands, I shall be able to be thrifty.'

Épernon, however, was still not off his hands. The Duke's growing opposition to and hatred of Guise had made him refuse the marriage planned for him—Christine of Lorraine was Guise's cousin—and the alternative plan of marrying Navarre's sister had broken down because of the intense hostility of the Parisians when they heard it merely rumoured.

'They suspect,' wrote the Imperial Ambassador, 'that the Duc d'Épernon is to marry the sister of the King of Navarre and that in favour of this alliance the King is about to create Épernon Constable of France and that the King will be reconciled to the King of Navarre and maintain his pretensions to the succession.'

Épernon had, in fact, no intention of committing himself irrevocably to the Huguenots and was examining the possibility of a marriage which would ally him with the great house of Montmorency, leader of the *Politiques*—those lukewarm Catholics who for reasons of political self-interest sided

47

with the Calvinists. But he was very definite in his advice to the King to accept the offers of help from England and Flanders and to appoint Henry of Navarre leader of all the Protestant forces to crush the League.

Joyeuse, on the other hand, was even more emphatic in begging Henri to do nothing of the kind, and he drew a vivid picture of the calamities likely to overtake France were there another civil war and a breach with Spain.

Henri, torn between their conflicting counsels, wrote to Joinville to ask Guise his political intentions. The Duke sent answer 'that it was never his intention to take up arms against the person of his sovereign and that he was and would always be His Majesty's humble servant'. His only concern was for the Faith which they both professed and the League was merely a weapon for enforcing it, which was entirely at the King's service.

Meanwhile the Cardinal de Bourbon left Gaillon for Péronne, as a symbolic headquarters, and from there published an official declaration. He professed the most devoted loyalty to Henri's person and emphasised that the sole reason for his being ready to take up arms was the overthrow of heresy. He invited the King to rely on M. de Guise and to put himself at the head of the armies of the League. The question of the succession was modestly and distantly alluded to and the manifesto concluded with a magnificent tribute to the Queen-Mother 'to whose indefatigable labours, which I myself have shared, France owes her salvation and our holy religion its preservation'.

Henri replied by a counter-manifesto imploring his subjects to beware of snares laid for them by designing men and asserting that if everything were left to his royal wisdom and clemency all would be satisfied. Épernon snapped at him:

'Instead of composing indifferent manifestoes, Your Majesty should act' and retired in dudgeon to Metz, of which he was Governor, to prepare for the fighting which he regarded as now inevitable.

Impressed by this, the King took action of a sort. He wrote to Navarre, bidding him be ready to come to his side; sent recruiting agents into Germany and Switzerland; forbade the sale of arms in Paris except to persons who gave their names and addresses; strengthened the guards at the gates of the capital and removed the captains and lieutenants of the citizen militia and replaced them by royal officers.

The League retorted by another proclamation in the name of the Cardinal de Bourbon[1] in which, after asserting attributable to the King, they declared they were ready to take up arms to restore the unity of the Church, to expel unworthy favourites and advisers from Court, to prevent further troubles by settling the succession and to provide for regular meetings of the States-General. And, to attain these objects, they swore to persevere 'until they should lie heaped together in the grave reserved for the last Frenchman fallen in the service of God and his country'.

To make it clear that this was no empty threat, Guise moved at the head of 12,000 troops to Châlons-sur-Marne as a convenient headquarters and fetched the Cardinal de Bourbon (whom he privately referred to as 'le petit homme' and others as 'l'âne rouge') in state from Péronne. The Cardinal, riding behind the banner of Guise with its blazon of eaglets and its motto: 'Chacun à son tour', had no doubt that everything was being done out of respect for him as the future Charles X. He only hoped that the Queen-Mother, whom he dreaded while

---

[1] It was signed by him alone, but there was circulated with it a list of the chiefs of the League which included all the Catholic princes of Europe.

he rendered homage to her, would approve.

For Catherine de Medici had decided that things had gone far enough and that she must again take upon herself the burden of negotiation. She was sixty-six now and suffering agonies from gout which rendered her left arm almost useless. She had persistent earache and toothache. She was so weak from a chronic cough, a stitch in the side and increasing corpulence that she could not leave her bed for days at a time. But the indomitable woman never weakened in her will and determination and when the Cardinal de Bourbon explained that he was too ill to come and see her, she threatened to be put in her litter and carried to see him.

In the circumstances, he admitted defeat and agreed to meet her at Châlons whither she painfully set out with the remark: 'Je m'en vais faire les doux yeux à M. le Cardinal de Bourbon.'

5

Sack and Cuirass

The Cardinal de Bourbon had all his life been an assiduous courtier and Catherine, in particular, had exercised a fascinated control over his weak and vacillating nature. In her tenacity of purpose and political acumen he had a glimpse of how he himself might have behaved had his will equalled his desires. And now, as he once more stood face to face with her, he capitulated immediately.

Catherine described their meeting in a letter to the King: 'The Cardinal de Bourbon arrived here yesterday a little before supper-time. He wept and sighed very much indeed while I held him in my embrace and showed his regret at having taken up these matters, all of which he talked about at some length. When I remonstrated with him, he frankly confessed he had committed a great folly. One must, he said, commit one such in one's lifetime and this was his.'

Guise was a different matter. If he too shed tears, the cause was physical. The famous scar, according to a diarist, 'made him very prone to tears, so that he presented two aspects, smiling with one eye, weeping with the other'. When he ceased to smile, the effect was inevitably grim, and the

Cardinal de Bourbon's attitude was enough to account for considerable gloom. 'I cannot tell you,' he wrote to his brother Louis, 'how inconstant and changeable is *"le petit homme"*. I am nearly beside myself with the trouble he is giving me.'

Catherine, reporting on Guise's arrival, noted that 'as he bowed low before me, he struck me as very melancholy and when we had begun to talk, the tears ran down his cheeks. After I had made the remonstrances which seemed fitting and promising him your pardon if he would only deserve it, I told him that his action served rather to weaken the Church and destroy it than to root out heresy and I spent much breath in showing him what experience has taught us—that peace has decreased the number of Huguenots more than any war. But he kept his own counsel in spite of every argument and remonstrance I could think of.'

Their discussions were inconclusive largely because they started from different premisses. Guise argued from the point of view of fidelity to the Church, Catherine of loyalty to the Crown. After ten days, she wrote to the King: 'The essential thing is to do away with this pretext of religion, which every chance agitator uses, and to substitute the question of loyalty; otherwise the first malcontent that comes by will force us all to take up arms.'

Nothing she could do would shake Guise. On May 20, she reported: 'The Duc de Guise came to find me on the way to Mass at Notre Dame de l'Épine and his face showed me he was sadder than usual. I let him say all that he wanted, but for a long time he only half-talked and when I pressed him for the reason for his doings, he answered rather coldly. I do my best to cause division between them all, but M. de Guise is just like a schoolmaster. He gives every excuse he can, yet he said to me that he did not know what plunged him into this business. He says that as he has devoted himself to the public good, the public must be satisfied.'

Catherine retorted by requesting Guise to attend to his own affairs and to leave the welfare of the realm to those responsible for it. But he remained unyielding and, on June 20, the Queen-Mother was driven to sign at Nemours (to which she had retired as being better suited to her health than Châlons) a treaty which conceded all the demands of the League. Previous Edicts of Toleration were revoked and *la religion prétendue réformée* was forbidden. Henceforth there would exist only one religion in France, the faith of the Catholic, Apostolic and Roman Church. Heretics were to be pronounced incapable of holding any office and those who refused to conform within six months were to be banished.

As a guarantee that this policy would be carried out, nine fortified cities were to be handed over to the League—Soissons to the Cardinal de Bourbon; Toul, Verdun and St. Dizier, the keys of the eastern frontier, to Guise; Dijon and Beaune to Mayenne; Dinan to Mercoeur, the Queen's brother; and to the Guises's uncles, Boulogne to Elboeuf and Rue to Aumale.

Festivities to celebrate the signing were obviously out of place, but with the relaxation of the tension Catherine's ladies-in-waiting staged an impromptu charade by dressing as men, while the Cardinal de Bourbon, with a veil made out of bed-curtains, disguised himself as a woman and, approaching on the arm of Madame de Simier, was solemnly presented to the Queen-Mother. He tactfully joined in the general merriment but privately he considered that Catherine's peals of laughter which became almost hysterical were a little excessive.

The messenger who had carried the letters and messages

between Henri and Catherine during the negotiations was the King's physician, Miron, who had been chosen because he was now the only man Henri unreservedly trusted. When he returned to Paris with the final draft, the King asked him his opinion of it.

'I am a doctor,' said Miron, 'and it is fortunately not my duty to have an opinion on such matters.'

'Then in friendship,' said Henri, 'imagine yourself my colleague; for am I not the physician who must prescribe for the body politics? Is not this too drastic a remedy?'

'Only time can tell, sire. But even if it kills the patient, you are bound to administer it. You have no choice.'

'The final word is mine.'

'To speak, yes. To determine, no. You cannot doubt that the Queen your mother has done all that is possible.'

'That's true enough. She must have been driven into a corner, for she'd never have done it willingly. In the last twenty years, she's been behind seven treaties.' He ticked them off on his fingers. 'Amboise, Longjumeau, St. Germain, La Rochelle, Chastenoy, Bergerac, Fleix—all for toleration. The first thing she taught me about governing was that a King must never take sides. And now she's reversed all the treaties and made me side with Guise. Poor soul!'

'What else could she have done? She has nothing to bargain with. You are on foot; Guise is on horseback.'

'Yet it has been known for infantry to win a battle.'

'Then let me put it another way,' said Miron.

Henri was wearing, as nowadays he often did, the habit of a religious order he had founded two years earlier, the Congregation de l'Annonciation de Notre Dame,—a cassock, loosely cut, made of coarse sacking with wide sleeves and a rope girdle.

Miron shook one of the sleeves. 'Your Majesty's sack,' he said, 'is not proof against the cuirasses of the League.'[1]

A fortnight after the signing of the Treaty of Nemours, the three Guise brothers, with the Cardinal de Bourbon, arrived in Paris for the ceremony of its ratification by the Parlement. Henri met them on the staircase of the Louvre as if they were his dearest friends, embraced them repeatedly and was gracious, even charming, in his conversation during dinner. With engaging honesty, he admitted: 'I signed the last edict against my conscience but very willingly because it seemed to me that toleration tended to the good of my poor people. I shall sign this new edict according to my conscience but against my will, for I fear it may prove the ruin of my realm. In destroying the *Prêches*, we may be endangering the Mass.'

As they returned from the Palais de Justice after the ratification, the Parisians shouted *Vive le roi!* It was so long since Henri had heard the cry that he suspected Guise of having bribed the crowds to raise it.

The King continued to exert all his considerable charm to win Guise's trust. He had decided on his course of action, of which the prerequisite was to put the Duke at his ease and to dispel his suspicions. Yet no one was deceived. One of Guise's

---

[1] Though at the foundation of the Congregation on 25 March 1583 the Cardinal of Guise had borne the crucifix in front of the outdoor procession (in torrential rain) and Mayenne had followed immediately behind the King scourging the royal back, the Duke of Guise had refused to have anything to do with it, but merely watched it somewhat contemptuously from a window. He was suspected of having circulated the verse:

> Après avoir pillé la France
> Et tout le peuple dépouillé,
> N'est-ce pas belle pénitence
> De se couvrir d'un sac mouillé?

'The King's sack' became proverbial in Paris.

friends warned him bluntly of the danger of assassination.

'Watch as you will,' he said, 'there will be a time when you will be off your guard, when you will have no weapons but your valour and reputation and these will not be enough to save you.'

'The King has a good heart,' replied Guise, 'and I am not afraid. After all, we have been companions from our childhood.'

But it was noticed by one of the Italian envoys at Court that the Duke 'had lost his habitual gaiety and that his hair was turning white at the temples'.

Henry of Navarre also went white. When the news of the ratification of the Edict reached him, he recorded: 'As I sat deep in thought upon this matter, my head leaning on my hand, my apprehension was so acute that it turned the half of my moustache which was covered by my hand snow-white.'

Navarre realised that, unless he now returned to Catholicism —which would have resolved the whole crisis except a family bickering between him and his uncle as to which of them was the true heir-presumptive—he would inevitably be once more formally excommunicated. On the other hand, if he remained a Huguenot, there was always the chance that the 30,000 German *reiters* under John Casimir, combined with the English and Dutch levies, might defeat the French troops and make him King in Henri's place. He decided to take the risk.

The expected Bull of Excommunication was published at the Vatican on 21 September 1585 and laid down that Henry King of Navarre and his cousin Henry Prince of Condé had relapsed into the heresies they had solemnly abjured, had taken up arms against the King of France for the purpose of carrying out a bloody persecution of Catholics, and must thus be held to be notorious and relapsed heretics who *ipso facto* forfeited their rank and sovereignty. The Pope, claiming 'the authority, surpassing that of all terrestrial kings and princes, given by God to St. Peter and his successors' then declared the sword of vengeance unsheathed against those two 'children of wrath, a bastard and detestable generation of the House of Bourbon'. Their subjects were released from their oaths of fidelity and commanded to 'render them neither service nor obedience, under pain of being included in the anathema pronounced on the princes'. Henri III, in virtue of his coronation oath which bound him to destroy all heresies, was exhorted to carry out the sentence.

The Pope's reasoning which led to this singularly inopportune pronouncement was, in theory, sound enough. He assumed that there were only two parties in France, the attackers and the defenders of the Faith. If the League would unite under the banner of the King and direct the forces of Catholicism to secure the enforcement of the new Edict, there would be no question of war, the problem of the succession could be solved peacefully and France would be safe. The Pope's mistake lay in supposing that Henri intended to ally himself with Guise for an hour more than he was forced to. Left to himself, the King would have preferred Navarre. The only genuine force for Catholicism was the League and in the 'War of the Three Henries' about to start Henri of Valois could be presumed to wish to align himself rather with Henry of Navarre than with Henry of Guise.

Meanwhile Navarre replied to the excommunication by ordering one of his pamphleteers to write and to affix to the statue of Pasquino in Rome a squib stating that 'Henry, by the Grace of God, King of Navarre, opposes the declaration of Sixtus V, calling himself Pope of Rome, maintains that it is false and, as touching the crime of heresy, sustains that

Sixtus V calling himself Pope has falsely and maliciously lied and that he himself is heretic and Antichrist. And he calls upon all the allies of the Crown of France to join him in opposing the tyranny and usurpation of the Pope and the League, enemies of God, the State, the King and of the general peace of all Christendom.'

6

Mary Queen of Scots

The English embassy which came to France officially to bring King Henri the Garter and secretly to urge him to support the Protestant rebels in Flanders had, among other diplomatic business, to press on Queen Elizabeth's behalf for the arrest of Thomas Morgan, the confidential secretary of Mary Queen of Scots. Accordingly, on 1 March 1585, the day after the Garter ceremony, Morgan was sent to the Bastille.

His imprisonment, however, was anything but severe. Henri had no desire to make his sister-in-law's[1] lot worse by appearing to side with her enemies, even if he diplomatically accommodated the Queen of England. He allowed Morgan two crowns a day for his prison expenses and permitted as many daily visitors as he wanted.

Morgan, who was now forty-two, had been introduced by Cecil, Elizabeth's chief minister, into the household of Mary Queen of Scots' gaoler when first she came to England and the Welshman had so completely gained her confidence, by various services he had rendered her and information he had secretly given her, that she had put him in charge of all her

[1] Mary's first husband had been Henri III's eldest brother, King Francis II.

correspondence. Eventually he had gone to Paris with a warm letter of recommendation to her cousin, the Duke of Guise, and her Ambassador in France, the Bishop of Glasgow, asking them to employ him in her service as a person eminently worthy of trust. They were to give him a pension of thirty crowns a month from her estate as Duchess of Touraine. Morgan did not despise this, though the English government considered his services worth four thousand crowns as well as considerable landed property. He was one of their best secret agents.[2]

Guise, from the outset, instinctively distrusted both Morgan and his intimate friend and co-worker, Charles Paget. It was reported in Rome that 'the Duke of Guise and the Archbishop of Glasgow did not consider those two men as trustworthy, fearing that they hight hold secret correspondence with some of the Council in England, though the Queen of Scots trusted greatly in them contrary to the wish and opinion of the said Duke'.

The official English request for Morgan's arrest was intended to allay Guise's suspicions by demonstrating—it was hoped—the spy's fidelity to Mary Queen of Scots and the hostility he naturally suffered on that account from the English Government. But though it deceived King Henri it did not alter Guise's attitude.

From Elizabeth's point of view, it was particularly important that Morgan should be completely trusted by Mary and her supporters. He formed an essential link in a new plan to entrap the Queen of Scots in a dangerous correspondence. An Act had just been passed providing the death penalty for anyone in

[2] This fact, though long suspected by historians, was finally established only in 1964 in a work of monumental scholarship (it has over 750 footnote citations of documents) *An Elizabethan Problem* by Leo Hicks.

whose favour any plot against Queen Elizabeth was undertaken, whether or not that person was cognisant of it.

Thus, if it could be established that a conspiracy or rising had as its object the placing of Mary Queen of Scots on the throne by the elimination of Elizabeth (for, though only Catholics considered Mary the rightful occupant of the throne of England, no one questioned that Mary was the rightful heir to it after Elizabeth's death), then, even if Mary were in total ignorance of the plans on her behalf, she could be legally put to death. The new Act was, and was intended to be, the Queen of Scots' death-warrant, for it could only be a matter of time before some attempt would be made to release her. And Mary understood it as such.

During her sixteen years of imprisonment in England[3] she had expected death often enough. For her, the matter now became not even when she would be killed. What troubled her was why she would be killed. Would she be allowed to die as a martyr for the Catholic Faith, of which, in a sense, she was the European pivot? Or would she be somehow enmeshed in a pretended plot by which she might be made to appear an accomplice to murder?

The same alternative faced Elizabeth who was determined that, if it were by any means possible, Mary should be regarded as a murderess. And it was for this end that the services of Thomas Morgan were now required.

To render the Queen of Scots more vulnerable to their plans against her, Cecil and Walsingham, the Government's spymaster, made her imprisonment more severe. All her private letters were stopped. Her place of imprisonment was changed

[3] The Calvinist rebels, under her half-brother, Moray—aided by Queen Elizabeth—had driven her out of Scotland and, at Solway Firth, the boatman, instead of taking her to France as she had wished, had landed her in England. See *The Florentine Woman*, p. 174.

to a damp and draughty castle standing by a marsh which exhaled poisonous fumes. A new gaoler was appointed, a bigoted and sadistic Puritan who hated Catholicism—and her as a royal representative of it—beyond measure. He was ordered to confine her so strictly that she was not even allowed to take the air. The canopy above her chair, the symbol of her royalty which on that account she prized, was rudely taken down and every possible insult heaped on her. By such means it was hoped that when she was next permitted to receive a letter to lessen her loneliness she might accord it an unqualified welcome.

By the autumn of 1585, Mary's health had become so bad and she herself so weak that Elizabeth felt bound to give heed to the protests of Henri III against the barbarous treatment of his sister-in-law of which his ambassador in London was indignantly informing him. The Queen of Scots was accordingly, though left in charge of the same unsympathetic gaoler, moved to a more civilised place of confinement, a manor house a few miles away. It was here, on 16 January 1586, that to her astonishment and delight she received a letter from Morgan which he had written from the Bastille three months earlier.

May it please Your Majesty, many have found the means to visit me in this undeserved captivity of mine; and among others there was with me of late one named Gilbert Gifford, a Catholic gentleman to me well known, for he was brought up in learning on this side the seas. He is returning to his country and offered to do me all the friendly offices he may do. He required my letters to Your Majesty to give him credit and a means to enter intelligence with Your Majesty. For this purpose I have

62

given him these few lines, assuring myself of his faith and honesty. I hope he will show his good will and diligence in the cause and that somewhat may fall out to Your Majesty's advantage.

This I desire as God knoweth, who knoweth my heart and that I have no other desire in this life but to serve God, Your Majesty and my country. Thus with my prayers in this captivity for your preservation and consolation, I most humbly take my leave and commit Your Majesty to God, Who ever preserve Your Majesty.

Written this 15th of October.

> Your Majesty's most humble and obedient
> faithful Servant, during life to command,

—

X

Gilbert Gifford was in his twenties but his appearance was that of a wide-eyed, somewhat naïve boy in his teens. His temperament was such that he liked spying for spying's sake. As the son of a Catholic family he had been educated abroad and had entered the English College in Rome to prepare for the priesthood. His preceptors, however, understood his nature and threw him out. He thus seemed to Walsingham's secret agent in the College a promising candidate for the spy-service, but Walsingham, at that point, considered Gifford too impetuous to be useful. It was only recently, when Gifford managed to enter the Jesuit college at Rheims, that the English authorities decided that, despite his appearance, he might be mature enough to be trusted. Walsingham was now awaiting him with some interest.

When Gifford arrived in England he went to stay with one of Walsingham's most valuable agents, Thomas Phillips, a man of thirty, small, 'slender every way' and pockmarked.

Phillips was an expert forger; he was fluent in French and Italian and he had the rare gift of being able to break almost any cipher. Like Gifford, he had a passion for spying and took pleasure in destroying people, and, on that account, Walsingham could trust him implicitly.

Gifford had the immediate *entrée* to English government circles, but what was important in the context of his work was his ability to gain the confidence of the French Ambassador. He had various letters of credit to introduce him (including, naturally, one from Morgan) testifying to his honesty and fidelity to the Catholic Faith and the Queen of Scots. He had, so he told the Ambassador, been sent to England by the Queen's servants in Paris and he had undertaken solely *à cause de la religion* to organise a secret post by which the Queen could communicate with the outside world again. The Ambassador, despite some misgivings on the ground of Gifford's youthful appearance, accepted his assurances.

The first step in the organisation of the secret post was entrusted to Phillips. He approached the brewer who regularly delivered beer to the Queen of Scots' household and who was known to be sympathetic to her and suggested to him that —for a consideration—he might care to render a special service to Her Majesty of Scotland. The brewer agreed and undertook that when a 'secret party', an agent of the Queen of Scots, should deliver some letters to him, he would enclose them in a corked tube and slip it through the bung-hole of one of the casks he was delivering to her household. In the same way, when he collected his empties, he was to look for the tube and deliver it to the 'secret party' who would be in the neighbourhood to receive it.

Everything was now reduced to an efficient simplicity. Mary's correspondence was known in every detail to the

English Government long before the recipients of her letters received them. The brewer, meaning no evil, delivered the tube containing them to Gifford—the 'secret party'—who gave them immediately to Phillips. Phillips deciphered them and sent a copy *en clair* to Walsingham. The letters were then resealed by Arthur Gregory—an expert in that particular art kept by Walsingham and referred to affectionately as 'Arthur' —and taken by Gifford to the French Embassy, whence they were sent to France under diplomatic immunity. Incoming letters were similarly treated in the interval between Gifford's collection of them from the French Embassy and his delivery of them to 'the honest man'—as they called him, not altogether in irony—the brewer. The trap was perfect. Walsingham's spy-service was the best in Europe and this was one of his masterpieces.

The only untoward circumstance was the complete absence of anything in any of the letters which could possibly be twisted to serve Elizabeth's purpose. It therefore became necessary to find some desperate Catholic plotters who would make an attempt to rescue Mary and would also take her into their confidence. At the end of April 1586, when the post had been established three months and yielded nothing of interest, Walsingham sent Gifford to Paris to consult Morgan. He returned with the name of Sir Anthony Babington.

Babington, a twenty-five-year-old Catholic gentleman 'of enchanting manners and wit' and a reasonable fortune, had been a page to Mary Queen of Scots' first gaoler, the Earl of Shrewsbury, at the time when Morgan was his secretary, and he had retained a romantic devotion to her. Babington, during a visit to France before he entered as a student in Lincoln's Inn, had seen Morgan again and been told of the Spanish-Guise plans for releasing Mary Queen of Scots and impressed with the necessity of raising an insurrection among the English Catholics when the invasion took place. He had, however, done nothing about it but discuss it romantically with a few intimate friends, and at the moment, seeing no chance of a Catholic being able to enjoy a tolerable life or to practise his religion in England, he was considering emigrating permanently to Italy.

He was in this mood when Gifford returned from France and introduced himself to Babington as the friend and confidant of Morgan, bearing important news. The invasion would take place within three months at most. Was it not dishonourable to think of leaving the country just at this moment when he might be able to do a great service to persecuted Catholics and especially to Mary Queen of Scots? Moreover, the Queen of Scots was relying on him and he would shortly be hearing from her.

Babington objected that she was in such close confinement that nobody could hear from her, but Gifford, wide-eyed and mysterious, told him to wait and see.

The letter duly arrived, addressed to 'Master Anthony Babington, dwelling most in Derbyshire at a house of his own within two miles of Wingfield'. Morgan had written to Mary advising her to get in touch with Babington, who in the past had rendered her certain services by having a letter delivered, and the Queen had done so with a short and colourless note.

Babington, advised, if not actually supervised, by Gifford, wrote a long and detailed reply.

'Most mighty, most excellent, my dread sovereign Lady and Queen, unto whom only I owe all fidelity and obedience', it began and proceeded to explain that 'upon the remove of your royal person from the ancient place of your abode to the custody of a wicked puritan, a mortal enemy both by faith and faction to Your Majesty, I held the hope of our country's weal, depending (under God) upon the life and health of Your Majesty, to be desperate. I thereupon resolved to depart the land, determining to spend the remainder of my life in such solitary sort as the wretched and miserable state of my country did require.

'The which purpose being in execution, and standing upon my departure, there was addressed to me from the parts beyond the seas a man of virtue and learning and of singular zeal to the Catholic cause and Your Majesty's service who informed me of great preparation by the Christian Princes (Your Majesty's allies) for the deliverance of our country from the miserable state wherein it hath too long lain.'

The crucial point, on which Babington wanted definite reassurance, was the foreign invasion. Without this there was little possibility of any rescue of Mary Queen of Scots. King Philip's intention of equipping a great armada against England had been talked of for years, but was the plan ever likely to materialise? Gifford assured him that he had had it from Morgan who had had it from the Spanish Ambassador himself that, by September at latest, 'the enterprise of England' would be undertaken.[4]

Babington continued his letter: 'When I understood this, my special desire was to consider by what means, with the hazard of my life and friends in general, I might do your sacred Majesty one good day's service.' The considerations he

[4] There is no need to suppose that Gifford was giving false encouragement, or that he did not himself believe it. Though the Armada did not in fact sail for another two years—the July of 1588—King Philip as early as the January of 1586 had completed his plans for it and the outburst of urgent preparations in ports and fortresses and arsenals and workshops and market-places throughout Spain, Portugal, Naples, Sicily and Northern Italy, had convinced many people (including Cecil and Walsingham) in that July of 1586 that an autumn invasion was a possibility.

put down for the carrying-out of 'the last hope ever to recover the Faith of our forefathers and to redeem ourselves from the servitude and bondage which heresy has imposed on us with the loss of thousands of souls' were

'First, assuring of invasion, sufficient strength in the invader.

Ports to arrive at appointed, with a strong party at every place to join with them and warrant their landing;

The deliverance of Your Majesty;

The dispatch of the usurping Competitor.'

The letter continued: 'Forasmuch as delay is extreme dangerous, it may please your most excellent Majesty by your wisdom to direct us and by your princely authority to enable such as may to advance the affair. Myself with ten gentlemen and a hundred of our followers will undertake the delivery of your royal person from the hands of our enemies. For the dispatch of the usurper, from the obedience of whom we are by the excommunication of her made free, there be six noble gentlemen, all my private friends, who for the zeal they bear to the Catholic cause and Your Majesty's service will undertake that tragical execution.'

This curious indiscreet letter surprised no one more than Babington when he considered it coldly. Most of it was not true. The 'ten gentlemen' and the 'hundred our followers' had no existence except in his imagination and of the 'six gentlemen' ready to kill Elizabeth, there was only one he knew—a lawyer in Barnard's Inn who had known Gifford in Rome and was inclined to accept with a narrow pedantry the proposition, disputed in most Catholic circles, that traditional formulae were to be taken *au pied de la lettre* and that excommunication justified assassination.

The hand indeed was the hand of Babington, but the voice was the voice of Gifford, who had pointed out that it was idle to write to the Queen without some concrete proposals and that, having asked for her advice and direction, he could modify them in any ensuing discussion.

As far as Gifford was concerned, he had done his work perfectly. The letter, establishing the existence of a plot to murder Queen Elizabeth, could, whatever Mary might reply, be used under the new Act as the Queen of Scots' death-warrant. Gifford had only one more service to perform. He collected the reply from 'the honest man' and delivered it to Phillips. That was on July 17. The same night, knowing the ways of his world and having no desire to experience the unkind fate which occasionally overtook those whose knowledge was considerable but whose utility was at an end, he crossed to France and was never seen in England again.[5]

When Phillips had deciphered the long reply of Mary Queen of Scots to Babington's letter, he triumphantly drew a gallows on the outside of the *en clair* copy he sent to Walsingham; and Mary's gaoler, to whom Phillips had given the news, wrote a short letter of congratulation: 'Sir, God hath blessed your faithful and careful labours and this is the reward due for true and faithful service. Thus trusting Her Majesty and her Councillors will make their profit of the merciful pro-

[5] The rest of his career was short and chequered. He found himself under suspicion from Guise in Paris and, in an attempt to restore his credit, managed to get himself ordained priest. Unfortunately he was shortly after his ordination taken in a brothel and committed to the Bishop's prison. His lodgings were searched and his papers seized, much to the alarm of the English Ambassador who wrote in panic to Walsingham: 'They have letters of Phillips to him and mean to prove that he was the setter-on of the gentlemen in that enterprise of the Queen of Scots. Also that he was engaged for this by you, with Her Majesty's knowledge.' The Ambassador promised to spare no efforts to steal the incriminating letters—as 'being to Her Majesty's dishonour' —but he did not succeed. Gifford was left to rot in prison where he died towards the end of 1591, still well under thirty.

vidence of God, I commit you to the mercy and favour of the Highest.'

A week before she received Babington's letter, Mary had been officially given other news which had almost broken her spirit. Her only son, James, who was now nineteen and called himself King of Scotland, had finally betrayed her and signed a treaty with Elizabeth by which Mary and her interests were totally excluded and James, in return for a subsidy, became a pensioner of England. Though some months previously, when she had first had knowledge of his intention, Mary had written: 'I am grievously offended at my heart at the impiety and ingratitude that my child has been constrained to commit against me,' she had endeavoured to solace herself by blaming the betrayal on the 'constraint' of his advisers. Maternally, she still continued to deceive herself as to the real nature of the deplorable degenerate whom Darnley had fathered on her.[6] But now the last illusion was dispelled and in the depths of her misery and anger she lost her judgment. She brushed aside the entreaties of her devoted French secretary, Claude Nau, to leave Babington's letter unanswered.

Her reply to her 'trusty and well-beloved' would-be rescuer discussed his plan point-by-point as he had outlined it and it bore traces of the disturbance of her mind. She assumed 'the dispatch of the usurper from the obedience of whom we are by the excommunication of her made free' without questioning it, yet she wrote as if at the same time Elizabeth was to be left alive and on the throne: 'To take me from this place before being well assured to set me in the midst of a good

[6] He became, of course, King James I of England. The description of him in the dedication of the Authorised Version of the Bible errs on the side of flattery.

army were to give sufficient cause to that Queen in catching me again to enclose me forever in some hole from which I should never escape (if she did use me no worse) and to pursue with all extremity those that had assisted me.'

In spite of Phillips's triumphant gallows-mark, the long letter was not altogether satisfactory. It was, of course, true that the mere reception of Babington's letter, even if she had not answered it, made Mary under the new Act mortally guilty. But Elizabeth was uneasily aware that, in Europe, her *ad hoc* statutes were not respected by jurists. For instance, in the tight tyranny which was England, her enactment that the saying and hearing of Mass was High Treason was obediently accepted, but an astonished Christendom regarded it as eccentric, if not imbecile. In consequence Elizabeth invariably tried to prove, for the benefit of other nations, that the priests who were hung, drawn and quartered for their priesthood were also guilty of treason in the ordinary sense of the term.[7]

If this was important in the cases of the priests, it was doubly so in the case of Mary Queen of Scots. Elizabeth would have to justify her death to Europe and particularly to her brother-in-law, Henri III, whose alliance she needed against Spain. She was therefore desperate to be able to represent Mary as having taken active steps, as far as she could, to have her murdered. And this Mary's reply as it stood would hardly bear out in an impartial court of law.

Consequently Elizabeth suggested to Walsingham that Phillips (to whom she had just granted a special pension for his services) should forge a post-script which would put the

[7] There were, indeed, certain priests engaged in political plots. The importance of the recent (1970) canonisation of the Forty Martyrs is that these particular men and women, representative of hundreds more, after the most rigid historical examination of their cases, were shown to have died only for the Catholic faith and to have been innocent of any secular plotting.

question of Mary's active complicity beyond doubt. Walsingham, though he feared it might 'breed jealousy', obeyed and Phillips accordingly added to the Queen of Scots' letter an inquiry about the 'six gentlemen' who would be responsible for 'the dispatch of the usurping Competitor'.

'I would be glad to know,' the forged postscript ran 'the names and qualities of the six gentlemen which are to accomplish the designment, for it may be I shall be able, upon knowledge of the parties, to give you some further advice necessary to be followed therein, as also from time to time particularly how you proceed, and as soon as you may (for the same purpose) who be already, and how far, everyone is privy here-unto.'

With this, all preparations were completed. There only remained to spring the trap. At the beginning of August, while Mary, at her gaoler's suggestion, was allowed to ride on the moors near her place of imprisonment, she was met by a special messenger from Court who greeted her with: 'Madame, the Queen my mistress, finds it very strange that you, contrary to the pact and engagement made between you, should have conspired against her and her State, a thing which she could not have believed had she not seen proofs of it with her own eyes and known for certain.'

Mary was thereupon taken to another prison, her rooms in the old one searched, her possessions and papers confiscated and most of her servants taken from her. Three days later Babington and his friends were rounded up, and tried and condemned within a month.

On the night before the trial Queen Elizabeth wrote to Cecil commanding that 'when the judge shall give judgment for the manner of death it must be done in the usual form yet in the end of the sentence he may say that the manner of their death for more terror be referred to Her Majesty'.

Cecil replied that this was inadvisable because 'by protracting the due fashion of execution both to the extremity of the pains in the action and to the sight of the people to behold it, the manner of the death would be as terrible as any other new device could be'. He accordingly gave the executioner instructions that the prisoners were only to be given one swing of the rope before they were cut down so that they might be fully conscious—'alive and seeing' as an eyewitness put it—when they were castrated, ripped up and disembowelled. Babington himself suffered this in the first day's executions, but the crowd's reaction was not what the Government expected. The people were not terrified by the cruelty; they were indignant and angry and their demeanour was such that the original order was countermanded the following day. 'The Queen, being informed of the severity used in the executions the day before and detesting such cruelty' the official explanation ran, 'gave express orders that these should be used more favourably and accordingly they were permitted to hang till they were quite dead before they were cut down and bowelled.'[8]

On October 15 the trial of Mary Queen of Scots took place in Fotheringhay Castle where she had been finally imprisoned. At first she refused to acknowledge the competence of the court: 'As an absolute Queen, I cannot submit to orders nor can I submit to the laws of this land without injury to myself and all other sovereign princes. I do not recognise the laws of England.' But she changed her mind at the last moment—

[8] 'It is a sufficient comment on the famous Babington Plot' writes Alan Gordon Smith in his *The Babington Plot*, 'that this mean and cowardly official lie is so typical as to form a congruous termination to its history.' The apologists for Elizabeth justify her action on the grounds that she feared assassination; but, as Lady Antonia Fraser so rightly points out in her *Mary Queen of Scots*, 'this is to continue the propaganda of Walsingham successfully beyond the grave, since there was, after all, little real danger to Elizabeth from a plot vetted throughout by Walsingham'.

on the evening of October 14—because she realised that this was the crucial moment in which she could establish that her death was to be a martyrdom for her Faith. As she put it, she was playing her last rôle towards the theatre of the world rather than to the realm of England. She agreed to appear to answer the single charge that she had plotted the assassination of Elizabeth.

'I do not deny,' she said, 'that I have earnestly wished for liberty and done my utmost to procure it. In this I acted from a very natural wish.' But she denied absolutely that she had instigated the murder of the English Queen. 'Can I be responsible,' she asked, 'for the criminal projects of a few desperate men, which they planned without my knowledge or participation?' She demanded to see the original of her letter to Babington, but all that anyone was allowed to see was Phillips's copy of it with the forged post-script. She entirely repudiated it. 'Think you' she said to Walsingham, 'that I am ignorant of your devices used so craftily against me? Your spies have surrounded me on every side.' Then, to the Commissioners: 'If such have been his actions, my lords, how can I be assured that he hath not counterfeited my ciphers to bring me to my death?'[9]

As a matter of course Mary was found guilty and condemned to death. The sentence was confirmed by both Houses of Parliament at the end of October and a prayer to Elizabeth added, asking for the Queen of Scots's immediate execution. But Elizabeth, no less than Mary, was aware that 'we princes are set as it were upon a stage in sight and view of all the

[9] As the original letter was never produced, it is possible that in Phillips's copy more was forged than the postcript. Mary herself asserted in an oath taken on the Gospels that 'the points that concerned the practice against the Queen's Majesty were never by her written nor by her knowledge'. For a discussion of the evidence, see Gordon Smith *op. cit* pp. 275-279.

world' and she temporised. The consequences of the execution on European—and especially on French—opinion were incalculable. She preferred a private assassination and ordered Mary's gaoler to arrange it. But his strict Puritanism, which had prompted so many petty persecutions of his prisoner, was in this grave matter to Mary's advantage and he wrote back in indignation: 'I am so unhappy to have lived to see this unhappy day in which I am required by direction from my Most Gracious Sovereign to do an act which God and the law forbiddeth. God forbid that I should make so foul a shipwreck of my conscience or leave so great a blot on my poor posterity as to shed blood without law or warrant.'

Elizabeth raged at his 'daintiness' and the 'niceness' of such 'precise fellows', but, for the time being, she let Mary live.

On November 1, All Saints Day, Mary accepted the fact that her death had been decided, and that it could not be long delayed. Deprived of her chaplain who, though in the castle, was not allowed to see her, she spent the day quietly in prayer and in reading the lives of the saints. Then she wrote what she supposed would be her last letters.

To the Pope she explained she had always tried to live in accordance with the Faith and practice of the Catholic Church as far as the conditions of her captivity had allowed and that now she was to be permitted, as the one remaining Catholic member of the royal house of England and Scotland, to testify on behalf of her religion by her death 'for my sins and those of this unfortunate island'. She also begged the Pope to uphold the arrangement by which, on her son James's desertion, she had transferred the inheritance of the crowns of England and Scotland to Philip of Spain.

To Mendoza, the Spanish Ambassador in France, she wrote:
'Praise God for me that through His grace I have had the heart
to receive the unjust sentence of the heretics with resignation
on account of the happiness which I esteem it to shed my blood
at the orders of the enemies of His Church, who do me the
honour to say that it cannot be subverted while I am alive.
Although I never committed act or deed tending to remove
Elizabeth from her throne (unless it be that they make a crime
of my right to the crown, which is acknowledged by all
Catholics), yet I would not contradict them, leaving them to
think as they please. This amazed them very much and they
told me that whatsoever I may say or do, it will not be for the
cause of religion that I shall die, but for having tried to murder
their Queen. This I denied as being utterly false, having never
attempted such a thing and leaving it to God and the Church
to dispose of this island in what relates to religion.'

In her long letter to Elizabeth she made one pre-eminent
request: 'Madame, for the sake of that Jesus to whose Name
all powers bow, I require you to ordain that when my enemies
have slaked their black thirst for my innocent blood, you will
permit my poor desolated servants to carry away my corpse
to bury it in holy ground with the other Queens of France,
my predecessors, especially near the late Queen, my mother;
having this in recollection, that in Scotland the bodies of the
kings, my predecessors, have been outraged and the churches
profaned and abolished; and that, as I shall suffer in this
country, I shall not be given place by the kings, your predecessors, who are mine as well as yours. According to our
religion, we think much of being interred in holy ground.
Refuse me not this my last request for the burial of this body
when the soul is separated, which, when united, could never
obtain liberty to live in peace.'

She repeated her wish for burial in France in her letter to Guise whom she made chief executor of her will and acknowledged as 'you whom I hold as dearest to me in the world'. Their common blood, their shared creed and their uncompromising loyalty made it possible for her to rely on him as on no one else. 'Although no executioner has ever before dipped his hand in our Guise blood, do not be ashamed of it, my dear friend, for a condemnation by heretics is profitable before God for the children of His Church.' She told him how her cloth of state had been taken away and how she had put a crucifix in its place. 'I showed them the Cross of my Saviour in the place where my dais had been.' Though she did not know that the Lorraine Cross was at the moment being placed on Paris altars, she was well enough aware of the significance of the emblem of their House: 'With God's help, I shall die in the Catholic Faith and maintain it with constancy without doing dishonour to the race of Lorraine who are accustomed to shed their blood for it. My heart does not fail me. *Adieu, mon bon cousin.*'

It was not till the afternoon of Tuesday, 7 February 1587 that she was told she must die next morning. The news was given her by the Earl of Shrewsbury and the Earl of Kent. They refused to allow her her chaplain to help her prepare for death but offered her a Protestant dean to clear her mind of 'the follies and abominations of popery'. Mary, though not disposed at that moment to enter into a theological argument, made such a defence of her beliefs that Kent exclaimed: 'Your life would be the death of our religion; your death will be its life.'

When the Queen heard this admission of the true reason for

her execution, she was overjoyed. She had won her last battle. She said: 'I was far from thinking myself worthy of such a death and I humbly receive it as a token of admission among the servants of God.' And when she was left alone again with her own attendants she returned to it. To her physician she said: 'Did you not remark what Lord Kent said, that my life would have been the death of their religion and that my death will be its life? How happy these words have made me! Here at last is the truth. They said I was to die for having plotted the Queen's death and now they admit that I am dying on account of my religion.'

As her chaplain was forbidden to come to her, she wrote out her last confession and sent it to his room by one of her women so that he might absolve her. Late at night she wrote her last letter to King Henri III 'to beg you as a Christian king, my brother-in-law and ancient ally, who have always protested affection, that at this time you give proof of your goodness: in the first instance by charity in recompensing my disconsolate servants with the wages due to them; this is a burden on my conscience that only you can relieve. Secondly, by having prayers offered to God for the soul of a Queen who dies a Catholic, stripped of all her possessions.' And to him again she repeated: 'I die innocent of all crime even had I been their subject. My Catholic faith and my adherence to the rights of this crown which God has given me are the two reasons for my condemnation. They will not, however, allow me to declare that I die for the Catholic faith. In truth I die because they fear for their own religion.'

The letter was concluded on the Wednesday morning 'two hours after midnight'. The execution was fixed for eight. To keep her mind from straying, Mary composed a rhyming Latin prayer:

78

O Domine Deus, speravi in Te!
O care mi Jesu, nunc libera me!
In dura catena, in misera poena,
Languendo, gemendo, et genuflectendo,
Adoro, imploro ut liberes me![10]

She rose early and when she was dressed went to her prie-dieu at a little distance from her ladies and took out the Host from the gold pyx she wore round her neck. St. Pius V, years ago, foreseeing her end, had sent her the consecrated Host with the unique privilege of communicating herself with It in the last moments of her life. Thus fortified, she rose from her knees and went proudly to her death.

As Elizabeth immediately closed all the English ports, the news of the execution of the Queen of Scots did not reach France for three weeks. When it at length became known in Paris, there was an explosion of popular indignation. 'The Leaguers,' wrote a diarist, 'shouted that she had died for the Catholic faith, in which opinion they were maintained by the preachers, who canonised her daily in their sermons.' The House of Lorraine had a new martyr and people began

[10] Englished by Algernon Charles Swinburne as:
O Lord my God
    I have trusted in Thee!
O Jesu my dearest one,
    Now set me free!
In prison's oppression,
In sorrow's obsession
    I weary for Thee
With sighing and crying,
And bowed down as dying,
I adore Thee, I implore Thee,
    Set me free!

seriously to believe the stories of the danger which Catholics ran by the continued existence of Huguenotism. Madame de Montpensier set up once more the enormous painting of Elizabeth presiding over the tortures of Catholic martyrs and the cemetery of Saint-Sévérin was crowded for days with those looking at it and listening to denunciations of 'the infamous English Jezebel'.

Nor was Henri spared. His lukewarmness on his sister-in-law's behalf, even though he had in fact made conventional protests through his ambassadors, was interpreted as collusion. Everyone knew that, had he threatened to break with England, Elizabeth would have been too terrified of being left without the French alliance at the mercy of Spain to have taken any measures against Mary. The people were indeed wrong in supposing that, as they spread abroad, Henri had actually suggested the death of Mary to the 'she-wolf of England'; but they were not wrong in thinking that Henri was not altogether displeased at the execution in so far as it was a blow at the Guises, and that it had had his tacit approval.

The requiem Mass for Mary was celebrated on March 12, in a Notre Dame draped in black. The King, the Queen, the Queen-Mother and the entire court as well as all the Guises were present. The preacher was the Archbishop of Bourges who had assisted at Mary's wedding in the cathedral twenty-nine years earlier. 'Many of us saw in the place where we are now assembled,' he said, 'this Queen on the day of her bridal, arrayed in her royal robes, so covered in jewels that the sun himself shone not more brightly, so beautiful, so charming withal as never woman was. These walls were then hung with cloth of gold. Who would have believed that such a change could have befallen her who appeared then so triumphant and that we should have seen her a prisoner, who had restored captives to liberty; in poverty, who was accustomed to give so liberally to others; treated with contumely by those on whom she had bestowed honours; that beauty which had been one of the wonders of the world faded in a dreary prison and at last effaced by a piteous death.'

The preacher turned to the reason for her death. 'She was accused of being a Catholic, of having come to disturb England and attempt the life of the Queen.' He scornfully rebutted the political charge and returned to the point Mary would have wished: *'Accusée d'être Catholique! O heureux crime! O désirable accusation!'* But this was not surprising. She was of the House of Lorraine, all the members of which were ready to lay down their lives for the Catholic faith.

The tension in the Cathedral was almost unbearable as he alluded to the Dukes of Guise and Mayenne, there in the congregation, as *'deux foudres de guerre'*. As soon as the ceremony was over, Henri sent for the preacher and, in a paroxysm of fury, ordered him to delete the passage in the published version of the panegyric.

7

The Sixteen

Three months after the requiem for the Queen of Scots, a new Papal Nuncio was appointed for France. His first task was to give the Pope a simple and unpartisan assessment of a situation which His Holiness was finding some difficulty in understanding. 'All around us,' he reported, 'are civil and foreign wars. There are factions of state and religion, factions of Catholics and Calvinists, factions of the *Politiques* and the League, factions of the most bitter type because they are between men closely akin. The nobles distrust each other; a few favourites are prosperous and proud; the hatred of the people for the Government is very great. The King is one man, yet acts like two persons. He is deeply religious, yet hates the Holy League. He wishes for the defeat of the Huguenots, yet fears it; he fears the defeat of the Catholics, yet desires it. These interior conflicts afflict him so that he lives in constant mistrust of his own judgment and trusts only in Épernon. The envy of Épernon for Guise has changed into hatred and the poison has made its way into the heart of the infatuated monarch. Épernon is the slave of his greed for possessions and honours; the heart of Guise is filled with liberality and humanity. Guise is adored by the people and hated by the King who loves Épernon who is hated by the people.'

Épernon made no secret of his advice to the King. He declared quite openly that 'in his judgment the King ought never to pardon the enterprises of MM. de Guise and the concessions exacted by them at Châlons'. He perpetually besought Henri to have Guise imprisoned in Vincennes and volunteered himself, with the 'Forty-five', to arrest him.

Guise was not unaware of his danger and when, on returning to Joinville at the end of May, he took his official leave of the *'vindicatif et dissimulé'* King, he said: 'I see that my enemies, sire, may wrest from me my honours and possibly my life. This might even occur during Your Majesty's lifetime. I intend, however, to show them that such a project will bring misfortune to them.'

Whatever the peril to him in the Louvre, in Paris itself the only danger to Guise was the overenthusiasm of the citizens, whipped to fury by the propaganda with which the Duchesse de Montpensier and the parish priests were surrounding the execution of Mary Queen of Scots. It was not merely that the cries of *Vive Guise!* which greeted his every appearance and the howls of execration which assailed Épernon on the few occasions on which, surrounded by the Forty-Five, he dared appear at all, invited reprisals. It was that the capital took the initiative and the people, fuming at the apparent inaction of the chiefs of the League, began to spin their own plots.

Municipal independence had always been prized by the Parisians and, to put an end to a state of affairs which was daily becoming more intolerable, the leading citizens now formed a new secret society. It had a governing body of sixteen, one representative from each of the sixteen *arrondise-*

ments of the city, and it was known in consequence as the *Seize*. The members were bound by oath to support the League, to do all in their power to ensure the defeat of the Huguenots and to make it impossible for a heretic ever to wear the crown of France.

The Sixteen were predominantly lawyers, merchants and clerics, but they also included the Keeper of the Mint, a prison official, a process server, a tin worker, a butcher and an auctioneer. They had a democratic tendency which was not entirely pleasing to the Lorraine princes and there was only one *gentilhomme* among them—the Sieur de Mayneville, the intermediary of the Guises—and he was not actually one of the Sixteen. Nevertheless, it was unfair to say, as his enemies said, that 'Guise had put himself in the hands of the *canaille* of the capital'. The Duke had put himself in no one's hands and, rightly, never doubted that he could control the wildest mob and enforce order, should it be necessary. What he could not do was to prevent them, in his absence, making plans of their own. Nor could he control his ebullient sister or bring her to reason.

Madame de Montpensier's inflammatory picture in the cemetery—though of that Guise fully approved—was the cause of the riot by which the *Seize* proved their strength. Shortly after Guise left Paris, Henri ordered that it should be removed and the curé of Saint-Séverin, who was exhibiting it, arrested.

On this news, the Leaguers sounded the tocsin, rushed to arms, occupied the bridge connecting the University quarter with the Right Bank and fortified a house in which they protected the menaced *curé*. They repulsed the Civil Lieutenant and a strong force of police and it was only after the King's Guard had been called out that the disturbance was quelled. Though Épernon strongly urged the King to arrest and hang the ringleaders, Henri thought it wiser to do nothing.

Madame de Montpensier's next plan was more ambitious. The Louvre was to be taken by the help of barricades in the adjacent streets, formed of barrels filled with earth and bound together by chains. The King was to be seized and taken to a house in the Rue St. Antoine which the Duchess had just bought for that purpose. He was to be confined in a little turret chamber and there vigilantly guarded until the *Seize* decided what was to be done with him.

When Guise heard of this, he sent de Mayneville to the Council of the *Seize* with the furious message that the choice of the method and the moment of protest was his and his alone and 'since they had presumed to doubt it, they might for the future manage their affairs as they liked as he himself would have nothing further to do with their concerns'. To his sister he sent an angry reproof and sarcastically asked her how she had proposed to proceed once she had got the King into the turret-chamber. She remained unabashed, but the leaders of the Sixteen made profuse apologies, humbly acknowledged their folly which they begged Guise to overlook and, in token of their contrition, sent him by de Mayneville a massive gold chain and 300 gold crowns towards the prosecution of the war.

Henri, still torn between Navarre and Guise and still hoping to effect either Navarre's conversion or Guise's complaisance, summoned the Duke to meet him at Meaux early in July. Guise suspected an attempt, once he was away from Paris, to assassinate him, but, as he wrote to Mendoza, the Spanish Ambassador, 'putting aside the doubt about my life, I have determined to start for Meaux at once, shutting my eyes to all risks, since the safety of the Catholic religion and the general welfare of Christendom is at stake. I intend to make the King speak out plainly and, by depriving him of every excuse for his pernicious designs, to make him continue the war.'

Henri received the Duke at Meaux with extreme graciousness and even Épernon, meeting Guise in the council chamber, 'embraced him as if they were the greatest of friends'. But the differences were irreconcilable. The King affirmed that he intended to enforce the Edict and allow only one religion in the kingdom. He added vehemently that such was his own private wish and conviction. Yet at the same time, he would be glad to 'purchase a good peace'.

Guise replied coldly that there was no way, as far as he could see, of obtaining such a thing without hurt to religion. Navarre had refused to return to the Faith and had made arrangements for a force of 25,000 German and Swiss Calvinist mercenaries to invade France on his behalf. Did Henri intend to make an accommodation with their leader, John Casimir, as he had done the last time they over-ran France in the Huguenot interest and forced him to a shameful peace? As for himself, said Guise, pointing to his famous scar which he had received when fighting them, he would risk a hundred more such wounds rather than submit to their intimidation.

He had, in saying this, struck the one note to which the King found it impossible not to respond. For Henri, however far he had allowed himself to be overcome by sybaritism and sodomy, had never lost his physical courage or the remembrance that, in his youth, he had been as great a soldier as Guise. And at the battle of Moncontour where, at eighteen, he was in command of the Royal forces against the Huguenots, he had seen the conduct of the German mercenaries and had on that account refused them quarter even when they fell on their knees and cried: 'Bon Papiste! Bon Papiste moi!'

John Casimir, son of the fierce Protestant Elector Palatine, had for years used his force of ten thousand or so *reiters* to great advantage to himself. He hired them out to anyone who would pay for them. Elizabeth of England had availed herself of them to help William of Orange in the Netherlands and Orange had used them on his own account. Coligny had called them into France to help him in the first Huguenot insurrection and had offered them the sack of Paris[1] as an inducement. In a later rebellion after Coligny's death, Navarre and Condé had called them in once more, in an effort to force Henri off the throne in favour of his younger brother, who was temporarily professing Huguenotism.

All the *reiters* asked was a basic payment and an unlimited opportunity to plunder and murder. 'They are very German soldiers and do spoil all things where they go,' an English Ambassador wrote of them. As their prime objective was pillage, they travelled with large, lumbering carts to carry their booty and, though cavalry, moved no faster than the infantry. Everywhere they went, burning, massacring, raping, plundering, destroying villages and trampling vineyards, they left a trail of bleak desolation. The people of France were, with reason, terrified of them and John Casimir found them a useful instrument for blackmail. Before calling them off from their last invasion in the Huguenot interest, ten years earlier, he had extracted from King Henri the Duchy of Étampes, the principality of Château-Thierry, nine lordships in Burgundy, a yearly pension of 40,000 *livres* as well as an undertaking to pay the *reiters'* arrears—which amounted to almost two million *livres* and entailed the pawning of the crown jewels.

[1] *See The Florentine Woman*, p. 114n.

In recalling this, Guise had put an end to Henri's indecision. The King spoke no further of an accommodating peace. Instead, he began to discuss the conduct of the war. They had three separate armies at their disposal. Henri himself would take the field and, with the army of reserve, defend the line of the Loire to prevent the junction of the German invaders and the Huguenots, while Guise defended the eastern frontier and Joyeuse held Navarre and Condé in check in the west.

The King was sincere enough in his intention to defeat the invaders, but he had by no means abandoned his determination to destroy Guise. He would now let events do it for him. A lengthy discussion with Épernon confirmed the possibility. Though he had promised Guise fifty *compagnies d'ordonnance*, the King would only actually provide him with half-a-dozen. On the other hand, he would see that Joyeuse commanded a force so well equipped that defeat was impossible. Thus, with any luck, Guise would be killed, though not before inflicting sufficient casualties on the Germans to make them pause; while Joyeuse would defeat Navarre so thoroughly as to make him amenable to the King's wishes.

Henri left Meaux so well satisfied with the cleverness of his plan that it became something of an obsession. On more than one occasion Miron noticed him laughing to himself and muttering: *'De inimicis meis vindicabo inimicos meos'*[2] and wondered whether the King really was going mad, after all.

---

[2] By means of my enemies I shall avenge myself on my enemies.

8

Defeat and Victory

The army which the King gave Joyeuse to command was sufficiently impressive to make Henry of Navarre, who was waging an indeterminate campaign of skirmishes, ambuscades and petty sieges in Poitou, consider it wise to retire temporarily into the Huguenot stronghold of La Rochelle. The news, however, that the Germans, instead of spending an appreciable time in attacking Lorraine, had crossed the French boundary and were making their way across Burgundy, made it imperative for him to attempt to join forces with them. In mid-October he started his eastward march, having as a rendezvous the source of the Loire, not far from Lyons.

In the evening of October 19, he arrived at the castle and town of Coutras, about twenty-five miles north-east of Bordeaux, which dominated the crossing of the river Drogne. He decided to cross at once during the night and immediately ordered the transport of some of his baggage and artillery. No sooner had this reached the other side than scouts brought news that Joyeuse was in close pursuit and would be *'en presence'* at latest by daybreak. Navarre, not daring to risk a crossing in the face of the enemy, recalled the artillery and spent the night in making a favourable disposition of his troops. His cannon he set on a sandy eminence which dominated the plain. A stream flanked him on his left, a warren on the right and in the ditch at the edge of the warren he concealed a long line of harquebusiers. Behind the sandy hill, the Butte aux Loups, and partly hidden by it, three cavalry squadrons were mustered for a final charge.

He had used his few hours priority to advantage. Joyeuse's troops, arriving half-exhausted from a forced night-march, would have to advance uphill over an uneven terrain in face of artillery fire, and unaware of the hidden harquebusiers.

Such mundane arrangements, however, were not considered enough. Duplessis-Mornay, who became daily more confirmed in his self-assumed rôle of the official Huguenot conscience, approached Navarre and in a voice loud enough to be heard by all around said: 'Sire, you know we love you; but we cannot answer to God for letting you lead us in a battle for Jesus Christ soiled by all the dirt you have wallowed in. It is not for me to detail the amours with which you have scandalised your followers. It will be enough to mention only the good citizen of La Rochelle on whose honoured house you have so recently brought shame by seducing his twelve-year-old daughter. You have caused enough grief to him and other God-fearing folk and before going into battle your men demand that you do public penance.'

Henry promised to consider it and when, at eight o'clock in the morning, the two armies faced each other and battle was about to begin, the King, riding among his troops, suddenly dismounted, publicly acknowledged his act, expressed his remorse, promised reparation and begged forgiveness of the family he had wronged. He then fell on his knees and prayed aloud for pardon from God, and all his army knelt with him.

Joyeuse, seeing from afar, said: 'Are they afraid? Why are they kneeling?'

'They are showing us,' said one of his *aides* who had been a Huguenot, 'that they mean to conquer or to die. Listen!' And, still on their knees, the Huguenot forces commenced to sing the Psalm: 'This is the day that the Lord hath made: let us rejoice and be glad in it' in the metrical version of Clément Marot:

> *Voici l'heureuse journée*
> *Que Dieu a faite à plein désir—*

When it was finished, they got to their feet, awaiting the signal to open battle, as Navarre rode over to his cousins, the Prince of Condé and the Count of Soissons, to say: 'Gentlemen, I need only remind you that you are Bourbons and, please God, I will show you today that *I* am the head of our house.'

The battle lasted only an hour. 'At nine o'clock in the morning,' wrote an eyewitness, 'the armies had scarcely struck a blow; at ten o'clock not a single man of the army of M. de Joyeuse held arms in his hands; they were all in flight or prostrate on the battlefield. The cavalry was first routed, then the infantry was defeated by the regiment called that of the King of Navarre.' Joyeuse's army lost about 2,700 men and the whole of their treasure and military store. But numbers were not the most grievous loss. Few battles had taken such toll of the flower of the youth of France. Joyeuse, within half-an-hour, realised that the battle was lost. When Saint-Luc rode up to him with the query: 'What do you do now?' he replied: 'Die at the cannon's mouth. A general has no other retreat.' He now lay dead on the field with his young brother,

St. Sauveur, and round him members of his *corps d'élite*, the Counts of Luze, Aubijoux, Graffot, Bellegarde, St. Suplice, Tiercelin, Tillac and la Bastide, the Captain of the Guard. Among the prisoners were Saint-Luc, Montigny, Cypierre, de Sansac, de Mareuil, Rochefort, Ville-gomblain, Montsoreau and the Marquis de Marguelé.

Navarre ordered the bodies of Joyeuse and his brother to be laid on the table of the dining-room of the inn of the Cheval Blanc at Coutras and, after shedding a few tears, gave them into the keeping of their relative, Turenne, ordering him to have them embalmed and transported to Paris or wherever King Henri should command.

Navarre had won the first Huguenot victory in their twenty-five years of warfare against the Crown and the effect on the morale of the Calvinists was inestimable. Militarily, the way to the east lay open and a triumphant meeting with the Germans could not be impeded. Politically, Navarre was now able to establish himself as not less important than Guise in King Henri's calculations. But at the moment of his triumph Navarre perversely threw everything away. The personal took its usual precedence. Next day, accompanied by a small contingent of cavalry, he left his army and rode not east but south to Pau to lay the twenty-two standards captured at Coutras at Corisande's feet. Nor, once he was with his mistress again, did he return to the fight for more than a year. Duplessis-Mornay was not alone in scathing reproaches for his sacrifice of 'the Cause' for this *'folie chevalaresque'*.

That same October, Navarre won a minor victory over his wife. Margot had not remained with him for many months after her return. She found his court dull and Corisande exasperating.

As one of her diversions, she one day rode with a small escort to visit Agen, one of her dowry-towns about twenty-five miles from Nérac, and decided to stay there. At first the citizens were delighted and flattered to have their Queen in residence and raised two companies of soldiers for her guard. She then wrote to Guise, formally joining the League; received reinforcements from him; built a citadel and declared war on her husband. Inconclusive and sporadic fighting continued for about six months until she became desperately short of money and antagonised the Agennois by her own amours and by the pillaging propensities of her troops. Her angry subjects rose against her and she was obliged to flee suddenly 'by the back door of the citadel', riding *en croupe* to her lover of the moment to take refuge with her mother.

Catherine, however, had at last had enough of her daughter. When the Queen-Mother heard of the investment of Agen, she had remarked: 'I see that God has left me this creature for the punishment of my sins through the afflictions which she gives me. She is my curse in this world.'

King Henri's comment to Catherine was: 'The more I think about it, the more I resent the ignominy which that miserable creature is bringing upon us. The best thing that God can do for her and for us is to take her out of the world.'

Margot, however, was not aware of this and was by no means prepared for her bleak reception. 'It was on my mother's assurance,' she noted in her diary, 'indeed by her orders that I took refuge with her and instead of the good treatment I had a right to expect, I found shame and annihilation. She brought me into the world; she now wishes to hunt me out of it. But patience!'

She needed her patience. Catherine, on King Henri's instructions, placed her under immediate arrest and sent her to the fortress of Usson in charge of the Marquis de Cavillac. Her husband welcomed the good news as he returned from Coutras to Corisande. But his satisfaction was short-lived. In a few weeks, Margot had seduced Cavillac and while he was visiting Lyons at her request she opened the gates to a strong troop of Leaguers whom Guise sent her at the pre-arranged moment. She was now able to barricade herself in her impregnable prison, to refuse entry to Cavillac when he returned from the errand on which she had sent him and to maintain her independence. She ruled Usson as its mistress, collected a herd of camels and, with her string of lovers selected from her squires, rode the countryside in search of suitable places for *fêtes champetres*. She wrote to the King for permission to import wine without duty, but he refused on the grounds that she might get drunk, fall off a camel and break her neck. Then he changed his mind in the hope that she would.

As for Navarre, his irritation increased. He informed Corisande: 'I am awaiting with impatience the moment when I get news that some one has sent some one to strangle my wife. That, together with the death of her mother, would make me sing the *Nunc Dimittis* with a full heart.'

The Germans, streaming their way across France, 25,000 strong, were too powerful for Guise to engage with the small army King Henri had allowed him. He therefore marched parallel with them, waiting for the opportunity for a surprise attack. This came at last towards the end of the following month when they had established their headquarters at Auneau, not far from Chartres. On the night of November 24,

Guise attacked with a body of 3,000 cavalry and, aided by the infantry which garrisoned the castle of Auneau which the Germans had not managed to capture, inflicted a decisive defeat on the invaders, who lost over 2,000 men, all their baggage and the plunder they had accumulated since entering France, their horses and nine standards.

The King, with Épernon, was in camp with the main army of 26,000 men, at Gien on the Loire and was in an excellent position to attack the Germans as, disheartened by their defeat and disillusioned by the conduct by their ally, Navarre, in leaving the war, they retreated homewards. But when Henri received the captured standards and the news of Guise's victory, he was so angry that he made an unprecedented refusal of the conventional gift to the bearer of good news. Both parts of the King's plan had spectacularly failed. Joyeuse was dead and Guise was, not only in Paris, the acknowledged hero of the day. When the *reiters* arrived in the neighbourhood of Gien, the King did indeed send Épernon to establish contact with them, though not to destroy them, as he easily could have done, but to conduct them safely to the frontier.

'Not only has Épernon placed himself between the *reiters* and me,' wrote Guise indignantly, 'but he has given them money to maintain the credit of the heretics abroad, and a thousand harquebusiers of the King's own guard and ten companies of *gens d'armes* to accompany their retreat. It is strange that Catholic forces are employed to recompense heretics for the damage they have inflicted on France. Every good Frenchman and true Catholic must feel outraged.'

From this moment it became clear that, whatever might be the King's intentions, it was the League and the League only which stood for France and for Catholicism. The point was reinforced, had it been necessary, by the King's return to

Paris just before Christmas when he attended a Mass of Thanksgiving at Notre Dame in great state, leaving it to be assumed that he was the victorious general, and forbidding Guise to enter the capital. The citizens, their eyes seeking vainly the towering form of Le Balafré, saw to it that the cries of 'Vive Guise!' drowned those of 'Vive le Roi!' and they sang pointedly: 'Saul has slain his thousands, but David his tens of thousands.'

In the streets there was a brisk sale for the latest pamphlet, a volume entitled 'The Martial Deeds of the Duc d'Épernon against the Heretics'. Every page was blank except for the single word *Rien*.

9

The Queen-Mother

When King Henri set out for the camp at Gien, he left his mother as Regent in Paris with the Cardinal de Bourbon as her adviser. It was the expected repetition of an old and tried pattern; but, this time, circumstances gave it a new dimension. For one thing, the status of the Cardinal had changed. He was no longer the conventional adviser of the crown and Catherine's long-standing 'gossip'. He was the Heir Apparent. And, more importantly, Catherine herself had altered. She was old—she had had her sixty-eighth birthday in April—she was ill and she was disillusioned.

All her life she had striven for religious peace but if she had advised concessions to the Huguenots it was because their political or military strength had made it inevitable. Recently she had bargained with Navarre at Pau and with Guise at Nemours, trying to persuade the one to change his religion and the other to moderate his demands. She had brought up Henri to see himself as king of all his subjects, whether Catholic or Huguenot, and she had never failed to try to strengthen him in this position. But she was now in a situation without precedent. Quite apart from preferring Guise to

Navarre as a man, she saw that to support the League was to support France against a foreign invasion which Navarre had invited. Nor had she the fear of Lorraine ambition which afflicted most of the court. The person she would have liked to see on the throne in succession to her son Henri was her grandson, the child of the Duke of Lorraine and her dead daughter Claude, and she had even discussed with Guise the possibility of circumventing the Salic Law to achieve it.

Another consideration which swayed her was that the 'middle' policy was now represented by Épernon, and of all her son's favourites, past and present, she detested Épernon most. She saw him not only as the greedy, grasping, arrogant Gascon that he was but as the symbol of the miseries of France. And more than any other single factor it was Épernon's hatred and jealousy of Guise that prevented the alliance of the King and the League which Catherine now believed to be necessary.

Her Florentine physician saw, perhaps, more clearly than she did when he told her: 'You say that Épernon is the obstacle to the reconciliation of Guise and the King, but, Madame, you know that if Épernon were to die, another and yet another Épernon would take his place.' She did not attempt to deny it, but neither did she explain that she still felt quite capable of dealing with Henri's *mignons* as a phenomenon. She had had no difficulty with Joyeuse. It was the actual personality of Épernon that was the stumbling-block.

Guise himself saw the situation with complete clarity. 'The King,' he wrote to his brother, 'having suddenly realised what forces we have within the kingdom, will try to deprive us of our strength by every means except force, which he sees is useless. He means to forestall us, to convict us of ambition and insolence if we take up arms and, if we do not, to wait till our means are overstrained, our adherents scattered by his disfavour and ourselves oppressed by the most careful and ingenious artifices he can invent. Either we shall be driven to make open war on the King or His Majesty will make war on us so covertly that we shall not be able to resist without appearing to put ourselves in the wrong and losing all our friends.'

In a situation sufficiently difficult, Catherine faced also a personal problem. To Henri she had given all her love; for Henri she would have given her life; and now Henri, swayed by Épernon, trusted her so little that she dared not counsel him directly. She wrote instead to his secretary: 'Sometimes the King does not interpret what I say according to my intentions and thinks that I am trying to palliate everything, either because I love Guise (which is as much as to say I love anything in the world as much as I do him, which is very hard for me to bear) or because he thinks I am a poor creature, ruled by a weak piety.'

At the same time, as she felt her strength deserting her and faced once more the formidable task of pacification, she, upon whom all her life so many had leaned, herself felt the need of support. And there was only one man in all France whom she could trust to give it to her. She called Guise *'le bâton de ma vieillesse'*.

Yet, before all, she kept faith with her son. She upheld Henri's ban on Guise entering Paris and when his cousin, Aumale, came to the capital she ordered him to leave immediately. He snubbed her with: 'Madame, I have not come to take the city, but only to order my spring clothes.'

She was happiest when, with single-hearted energy, she was able to organise the country against the invaders. She ordered the collection of all the grain in the countryside through which they would pass on their retreat and the storing of it in strongly fortified cities. The mill-wheels of all the grist mills were ready to be thrown into the rivers when they came in sight. The windmills were to be destroyed, the forges to be dismantled, the anvils removed, and all available salt to be put beyond their reach.

When the King came back to Paris at Christmas, Catherine could not leave her bed—though the Council was held every day in her room—but she asserted herself sufficiently strongly to make her son, despite his coldness towards her, admit the desirability of a *rapprochement* between Épernon and Guise. In due course, the favourite begged an audience of her, knelt before her bed, with his hat in his hand, and, in spite of her repeated requests to him to get up, remained in that position for an hour, assuring her that he was ready to be for the rest of his life her faithful servant and to do, in the matter of reconciliation with Guise, anything she asked.

She evaluated the gesture for what it was but took advantage of his mood to ascertain his real policy. What, she asked, was his confidential advice as to the course the Crown should adopt? Relieved that his answer corresponded with her own past policy and ignorant of her changed views, Épernon said: 'His Majesty the King, Madame, should make himself strong enough to fight either Guise or Navarre, as the need may be.'

He was quite unprepared for her angry retort: 'M. le Duc, I am now certain of what I have always suspected. You are nothing but a secret Huguenot!'

He vehemently denied it: 'Neither I, Madame, nor any of my family have ever been anything but good and faithful Catholics.'

'How can you expect me to believe that when you admit

that you would counsel my son, the King, to ally himself with the King of Navarre against M. de Guise?'

'With respect, Your Majesty, I said "as the need may be".'

'There can never be need for the Most Christian King of France to aid an excommunicated heretic against so true a Catholic as M. de Guise.'

'If that is Your Majesty's opinion—'

'It is, M. d'Épernon. What is more, it is the duty I shall enjoin on my son. And it is for you to accept it.'

She stormed on, according to a spectator, repeating that she was 'Queen Mother of the King and that there was no one who had more interest in the service of the King than his own mother, adding many threatening words to Épernon'.

The following month, the January of 1588, the chiefs of the League took counsel together at Nancy, the capital of Lorraine. There were present, in addition to Guise and his brother Mayenne, the Duke of Lorraine and his son Henry—the young man who was Catherine's choice for the succession to the throne—, the Dukes of Aumale and Elboeuf and a few of their most trusted followers. From their deliberations emerged a careful petition to the Crown. The essence of it was that the King should more strongly and openly support the League for the enforcement of the Treaty of Nemours by which he had pledged his royal word to ensure that only Catholicism be tolerated in France.

Among the eleven 'Articles of Nancy' was a demand that the decrees of the Council of Trent should be published and observed as a guarantee of the King's orthodoxy; that men suspected of sympathy with the Huguenots (Épernon was carefully not mentioned by name) should be removed from the Council; that all who had been confirmed Huguenots since 1560 should contribute a third and all Catholics a tenth of their property for the prosecution of the war against heresy; that the King should provide a permanent force to prevent another German invasion and—an attempt to widen the breach between Henri of Valois and Henry of Navarre—that all prisoners taken during the recent campaigns were to be offered the alternative of conforming to Catholicism within three months, after instruction, or being shot.

The King received the demands without any outward show of anger and merely deferred his reply until he had carefully studied them. Épernon's advice was immediately to arrest and hang all the leaders of the Sixteen so that Guise would be deprived of support in Paris. But Catherine said: 'My son, a wise man does not stir up a hornet's nest without first having covered his face.'

When the family conference at Nancy was over, Guise and his cousin Aumale went to Soissons—the town which had been allotted to the Cardinal de Bourbon by the Treaty of Nemours —from which Aumale exercised his Governorship of Picardy as Lieutenant for Condé. Aumale now petitioned that, in accordance with the policy of debarring Huguenots from office, he might be appointed to the post in his own right. Henri not only brusquely refused, but gave the Governorship to Épernon—the fourth new honour he had bestowed on the favourite since Christmas, when he had made him Governor of Normandy in succession to the dead Joyeuse. This public insult roused the Parisians to fury. Refusing to wait to ascertain Guise's own wishes, the *Seize* organised a conspiracy to seize the Louvre on April 21—the Thursday after Easter—and to bring Épernon to trial; to hold the King a prisoner and to proclaim the Queen-Mother as Regent once more; and to invite the Duke of Guise to come immediately to the capital as Lieutenant-Governor of the Realm.

The plot was betrayed to the King by his spy, Nicholas Poulain, but, for safety's sake, Henri left for Saint-Germain and Épernon left for Normandy early in the morning of the 21st.

Before leaving, the King sent an order to the Duchess of Montpensier also to leave the capital, as he was well aware of her 'treasonable and factious' proceedings. The Duchess, touching the golden scissors which she always wore at her girdle for giving Henri the tonsure sent back the message that His Majesty was completely misinformed. She was so enthusiastic a partisan that her greatest ambition was to be able to bestow on him another crown.

10

The Spanish Armada

Four days after King Henri left Paris for Saint-Germain—on Monday 25 April—a ceremonial event occurred in Lisbon which had a considerable effect on French politics. The Spanish armament assembled on the Tagus for 'the enterprise of England' was, after numerous delays, ready to sail, and its Admiral, the thirty-eight-year-old Duke of Medina Sidonia, went aboard his flagship, the *San Martin*.

Medina Sidonia was not the Admiral originally appointed. That honour had been given to the Marquis of Santa Cruz, the greatest sailor of the age, veteran of many campaigns, whom the Spaniards rightly revered as 'the light of war, the father of his troops, that valiant and unconquered leader'. But at the beginning of February, Santa Cruz had been taken suddenly ill and died and in his place, while all Spain mourned, King Philip had appointed Medina Sidonia for apparently no better reason than that he ranked second only to the Royal house.[1]

[1] The reasons for his choice remain a mystery. Scandalmongers suggested that his marriage to the daughter of the King's mistress, the Princess of Eboli, might not have been unconnected with it. In any case, this disastrous appointment alone was sufficient to justify Maurice Wilkinson's remark (in *The History of the League*) that 'the Armada had not the most remote chance of success from the day of its sailing'.

The new Admiral had no illusions about his total unsuitability for the post. While thanking King Philip for the great honour done to him, he begged to be excused from accepting it. He was not well enough for a sea-voyage. He had bad colds and suffered from sea-sickness. His conscience forbade him undertaking it for 'with such a vast armament and so important an enterprise, it was not right that it should be accepted by one who had no experience of the sea or of war'. He would have to take up a command without any knowledge of the officers, or of the men and ships, or of the plan of campaign, or of the correspondence which the Marquis of Santa Cruz had carried on for years. He would thus have to be guided by the opinions of others without being able to judge from his own experience what was good or what was bad or who was trying to deceive him. In short, if the King persisted in appointing him Admiral, he foresaw eventual disaster.

The King however was adamant and on April 25 after Mass in the Cathedral, the Cardinal Patriarch of Lisbon blessed the great silken standard, embroidered not with the lions of Léon, the castles of Castile and the lilies of Aragon but with a representation of Christ on the cross between the Blessed Virgin and St. John, and presented it to the kneeling Admiral. At that moment, the 1,200 harquebusiers, lining the streets between the Cathedral and the quayside, fired their muskets into the air, to be answered by three cannon shots from the ships on the Tagus. Medina Sidonia handed the banner to his standard-bearer and, walking beside it, headed a procession, which included representatives of all the nobility of Spain, to the quay where he took a barge to his flagship and from the deck watched the standard running up the halliards to the truck of the tall mainmast.

The fleet itself consisted of 130 ships, only eight of which were warships and the rest armed merchantmen of various sizes, including a considerable number of small coasting craft. It was by no means the 'invincible' armament of 596 ships that Santa Cruz had originally planned to make victory certain and at one blow to safeguard the Spanish trade with the Indies and to cut off English support for the revolt in the Netherlands.[2]

As the banner of the Crucified indicated, religion had become entangled with the economic and political causes of the war between England and Spain. Though the actual *casus belli*, which had, three years earlier, led to Philip's withdrawal of his ambassador from London, was the sack of Puerto Rico, San Domingo and Cartagena and the systematic plunder of Spanish traders on the high seas by Drake's piratical fleet of twenty-five ships fitted out with the help and consent of Queen Elizabeth, King Philip was inescapably involved in the international defence of Catholicism. Supposing that the projected enterprise should be successful, (and Philip more than most men was conscious that, as he put it, 'the result was in the hands of God Who gives or refuses victory as He will') the King laid down three conditions for peace— freedom to practice Catholicism in England; the return to Spain of the towns in the Netherlands occupied by the English and compensation for Spain's losses in the piratical English raids. The King would, however, be willing to waive a large part of his claim

[2] It is important to realise that, as Sir John Laughton puts it in his introduction to the *State Papers relating to the Armada*, 'nothing can be more inaccurate' than 'to represent the war as religious'. He continues: 'It is indeed quite certain that religious bitterness was imported into the quarrel; but the war had its origin in two perfectly clear and wholly mundane causes', the English raids on the Spanish-American trade and 'the countenance and assistance which had been given by the English to the Spanish king's rebellious subjects in the Netherlands.'

to such compensation provided the religious settlement was satisfactory.

Philip's actual terms were not, of course, communicated to the English people who instead were told by Cecil that one ship of the Armada carried a cargo of halters to hang them and another was loaded with faggots to burn them and that all men were to be killed, all women carried off into concubinage and all children branded with hot irons.

Independent observers were of the opinion that the Spaniards had little chance of enforcing either their real or their reputed objects. The Venetian Ambassador reported: 'It is commonly thought that, in spite of all the preparations, Spain will not attack England because the King knows full well how much the English fleet is to be feared, not only for its numbers, but also because the English have the reputation of being the best sailors in the world and great fighters at sea. The English fleet is waiting for the Spaniards and, if the battle comes off, it is highly improbable that the Spaniards would be able to land upon the shores of England in a condition to overcome the resistance they would meet there.'

What troubled Catherine de Medici about the Armada was Philip's precise purpose. She knew that Parma in the Netherlands was assembling munitions of war close to the border of Picardy. She assumed that the intention was either to invade England with Spanish veterans from the Netherlands while the Armada held the Channel or to drive the English from the Low Countries. But, she wrote, 'very often such preparations are made to fool those who are looking on so that it is worth taking pains to find out what is the real object of that great Spanish army'. What she feared was that the 'real object' was an attack not on England but on France.

She tried to get further information from the Papal Nuncio, by the device of informing him that in her opinion the best way of dealing with England's heresy was by a joint attack of Spain and France. This, indeed—she said—was what her son would have wished to do, if only he had peace at home.

The Nuncio, who knew perfectly well that if King Henri had any desire to intervene in the war it was on the side of England and that he had sent Épernon to Normandy to secure the Channel ports so that they might be available to Elizabeth's sailors, if necessary, replied bleakly that, if the King really wanted peace, all he had to do was to enforce his Edict with the help of the League.

Catherine objected that the situation, with the French Huguenots being able to rely on Dutch, German and English help, was not as simple as it seemed.

The Nuncio suggested that if France would help Spain in Flanders, Spain would be prepared to help France extend her frontier to the Rhine and thus to lessen the danger of another German invasion.

Catherine admitted that such a course might be worth consideration but argued that there was still the question of England. How, at this moment, could the King of France publicly renounce his friendship with Queen Elizabeth when it would result in so many French merchants in London being arrested and losing their capital? Besides, he had no way of defending the shores of France against the excellent English fleet.

Having at last brought matters to the point of this leading question, the Queen-Mother awaited the answer, either in denial or affirmation, which she could interpret to her satisfaction. Unfortunately, the Nuncio smiled, nodded and said nothing.

It seemed that Medina Sidonia would never sail. A fortnight after he had gone aboard his flagship he was still in the Tagus waiting on the weather 'as unfavourable as if it were December'. But on that day, Monday 9 May, Guise returned to Paris.

II

King of Paris

Guise left Soissons at midnight on Sunday 8 May accompanied only by eight of his gentlemen and Brigard, a merchant who had been sent to him with a message from the Sixteen imploring him to lose no time in coming to the capital. The King had returned from Saint-Germain, so the message ran, determined to exterminate the League in Paris. The royal army was in camp at Saint-Denis, dominating the northern suburbs. The Swiss Guards and the Scottish archers commanded the city itself. The Louvre had been turned into a fortified castle into which large quantities of arms and gunpowder had been introduced with a public flourish intended to intimidate the citizens. Everything was set for another massacre of Saint Bartholomew with, this time, the Catholic Leaguers as the intended victims.

The King, when his spies had informed him of the possibility of Guise's return to Paris, had sent Pomponne de Bellièvre to Soissons with an urgent and absolute prohibition. But before setting out Bellièvre had discussed the matter with Catherine, to whom for very many years he had considered he owed his chief duty, and he had discovered that she saw in Guise's return the only possible safeguard against revolution in the capital. No one but Guise, she was certain, could ride the storm. She did not, of course, countermand the King's order, but she made it so clear that she desired Guise's presence that Bellièvre thought it his duty to neutralise the ungracious message he had to deliver by the gestures, the intonations and the significant pauses with which he delivered it.

Guise replied 'that His Majesty's message was an implied reproof which deeply wounded his honour, but that, nevertheless, he would obey, provided the King promised that no harm or damage should come to the loyal citizens of Paris whose lives had been endangered by the aspersions of the King's counsellors and by their zeal for the Catholic faith'.

Guise had hardly returned this answer when he received alarming reports of the King's preparations not only from the Sixteen but from his sister, the Duchess of Montpensier, who urged him to return at once. Realising that he could rely on the Queen Mother's support and assuming that a private return with only eight of his suite could not possibly be construed by the King as in any way a challenge, he set off southward for Paris.

He arrived at the Porte Saint-Denis just after midday on the Monday. With his hat pressed low on his forehead and his face concealed in the folds of his cloak, he was not immediately recognised, but his great height and the princely bearing, so familiar to the Parisians, made a lengthy incognito impossible. Crowds had already started to gather before, at the corner of the Rue Saint-Antoine and the Rue Saint-Denis, one of his suite, as if in jest, removed his hat and drew the cloak from his face so that the scar was visible to all and said: 'It is time that Paris should know who is in her midst.'

The cries of 'Vive Guise!', tentative at first, grew to a roar. 'Guise is here! We are saved!' they cried. 'Vive Guise! Vive le pilier de l'Église!' They swarmed round him as if he were a saint, pressed their rosaries against him, kissed the hem of his cloak, rained flowers on him from windows and roof-tops. It was as if Paris had only one voice which shouted one name —'Guise!'

'Messieurs! Messieurs!' he called, 'c'est assez! C'est trop! Criez "Vive le roi!"'

But no one did.

He made his way not, as everyone expected him to, to his own Hôtel de Guise, but to the Queen-Mother's Hôtel de Soissons. The first person to catch sight of him was Catherine's favourite dwarf, Majosky, who was standing at the window describing the passers-by in terms which he hoped would make his mistress laugh. He was not having much success, partly because Catherine was attended by her god-daughter, the Duchess of Montpensier, whose *mots* were always more devastating than his. So when he suddenly screamed out that M. de Guise was just dismounting from his horse outside the main entrance of the Hôtel, Catherine supposed it to be an attempt to justify himself by perpetrating an outrageous joke and reprimanded him for lying. But Majosky repeated his information and the Queen-Mother's threat to send him to the governor of the jesters for a whipping died on her lips as a servant entered to inform her that Monseigneur le Duc de Guise humbly craved an audience.

'I was certain my brother would come, Madame,' said Madame de Montpensier.

'He could have chosen a better time, Catherine,' said her godmother.

She repeated this to Guise when he entered. 'I welcome you with all my heart,' she said, 'though my pleasure would have been tenfold greater at any other time.'

'Honour forbade me to wait longer to justify myself to the King.'

'Yet you present yourself to me instead of at the Louvre.'

'To have gone to the Louvre without having been summoned might have looked like contumacy. I have come to you, Madame, to ask you to use your good offices with the King your son to receive me in friendship.'

Catherine called her gentleman-usher, Luigi Davila, and sent him to find Henri's Grand Chamberlain, the Comte de Guiche. To him she entrusted the errand of informing the King of Guise's arrival and of inviting His Majesty to visit her at the Hôtel de Soissons.

The King had heard of Guise's arrival before de Guiche reached the Louvre and was discussing the situation with Villequier, the Governor of Paris, Pomponne de Bellièvre and the Abbé del Bene, Épernon's young catamite, son of the Savoyan Ambassador.

Henri's first reaction to the news was one of overwhelming anger: 'By God's Body, he shall die for it.'

Villequier and Bellièvre pointed out that it was unreasonable to suppose that, if Guise had had any hostile intentions, he would have come to Paris in the way he had and that it was probable that his visit would prove beneficial.

'I tell you, he shall die,' said Henri. Then turning to del Bene, he ordered: 'Find Colonel Alphonse and say I wish to speak to him at once.'

Villequier, who had once been one of Henri's *mignons* and by a strange convention had retained the right—though he seldom used it—to say whatever he wished, said: 'Indignation will do you no good. Do not speak of death. If Guise is harmed, the League will pull the Louvre down about your ears!'

'What a Governor of Paris I have appointed!' said Henri savagely.

When del Bene returned with 'Colonel Alphonse'—alias Alphonse d'Ornano, a Corsican swashbuckler whose business was assassination—the King said: 'You will have noticed that M. de Guise has defied my commands and returned to Paris. If you were in my place what would you do?'

'That, sire,' said d'Ornano, 'would depend on whether you consider M. de Guise your friend or your enemy.'

Henri drew his hand across his throat.

'In that case,' said the Colonel, 'if Your Majesty will give me the word, I will bring you either M. de Guise's head or his person before nightfall.'

'Thank you, my friend, I knew I could trust you. But I hope to provide other means.'

'And you, Father?' said Henri, turning to del Bene.

'*Persecutiam pastorem et dispergentur oves,*'[1] quoted the youth approvingly.

At this moment de Guiche arrived with the Queen-Mother's message, which threw Henri into a new paroxysm of fury. He answered her suggestion that he should visit the Hôtel de Soissons by a passionate negative and asked de Guiche how he presumed to mention so insulting a proposition. Was it not enough that Guise should disobey him by coming to Paris at

---

[1] 'I will smite the shepherd and the sheep will be scattered.'

all without him, the King, being asked to call on him as if he were a visiting sovereign? King of Paris, perhaps?

De Guiche replied mildly that Her Majesty the Queen-Mother's ailments were now giving her such pain that she had not been able to leave her Hôtel for three weeks and that doubtless she thought that His Majesty would wish to spare her the discomfort of even so short a journey as that from the Hôtel de Soissons to the Louvre.

'There is no need for the Queen, my mother, to accompany M. de Guise. He is more than capable of finding his own way.'

'As far as I could understand, sire,' replied de Guiche, 'Her Majesty seemed to consider it of some importance.'

'Then you will tell her that if she condescends to take the trouble of conducting M. de Guise to pay his respects to his sovereign I pray that she will take him to the room of the Queen my wife.'

'Yes, sire.'

'You understand?'

De Guiche knew that Queen Louise was confined to her bed with a slight attack of dropsy, but he was completely at a loss to understand why the King should choose to receive Guise in his wife's sick-room instead of his own cabinet. But, being a good courtier, he said: 'Yes, sire, I understand perfectly.'

As soon as de Guiche had gone, the King sent the Abbé to bring to him Laugnac, the Captain of the Forty-Five, with the principal five guardsmen on duty that afternoon.

When they entered his presence he asked abruptly: 'You remember the oath you have taken to me?'

'Yes, Your Majesty?'

'To obey implicitly whatever command I give you?'

'Yes, Your Majesty, to the letter and without scruple.'

'I can reply on you?'

'To the death, Your Majesty.'

'It is to the death of my greatest enemy.'

'In that case, Your Majesty,' said Laugnac, 'we will kill him for you with the greater enthusiasm. Give us our orders!'

The King outlined his plan. The six Gascons were to hide themselves in the small cabinet, occasionally used for private audiences, which adjoined the Queen's bedchamber. He would unlock the connecting door and leave it open so that they could hear all that was said. When he called out: 'You are a dead man, M. de Guise,' they were to rush in and kill the Duke.

Henri was delighted to notice that the men showed neither emotion nor curiosity. They said simply: 'Yes, Your Majesty' as if to assassinate the greatest nobleman in France at the foot of the Queen's bed (and she his cousin) were the most natural thing in the world. He could, he was certain, rely on them. Nevertheless, to make assurance doubly sure, he ordered the Scottish Guard to draw up in the great hall of the Louvre as on occasions of ceremony and the Swiss Guards, under *le brave Crillon*, most fearless and insolent of bravoes, to line the way from the portal of the palace to the gate of the draw-bridge.

Catherine came slowly through the streets in an open sedan-chair by the side of which walked the Duke bareheaded, wearing a white satin doublet and a black mantle and carrying his hat decorated with a large green plume. The crowds had not lessened. The roar of 'Vive Guise' was still the dominant note, but there were some cheers also for Catherine who had never lost her popularity with the Paris crowd. As they reached the Louvre, the Queen-Mother was oppressed by the sight of the military precautions and signalled to Guise that she wished to speak to him. He bent down to be within earshot.

'M. de Guise, you must promise me something.'

'If I can with honour, Madame.'

'You have vindicated that sufficiently by walking into this trap. I should have known my son better. After you have made your obeisance to him, you must leave the first moment you can. If it is possible, I will give you a sign.'

'What, Madame?'

'No more than this, M. le Duc,' said Catherine, looking him straight between the eyes.

While Catherine and Guise were talking to Queen Louise, Henri was in the adjoining room with the five murderers and Villequier who was making a last desperate effort to induce the King to change his mind.

'I tell you, Réné' said Henri, 'you are wasting your breath. Guise shall not live to brave me again. I will have his head on a pike before another hour is out.' Then, saying to Laugnac, 'strike well but not before I give the signal', he took a key from his girdle and unlocking the private door which opened close to the tester of the Queen's bed, he went to confront Guise.

The Duke, advancing at the click of the lock, made a profound obeisance, almost touching the floor with his knee, as Henri came through the door.

The King said angrily: 'What brings you here? I ordered you not to come.'

Guise drew himself to his full height and looked down compassionately on the hysterical king. 'I heard,' he said, 'that, by the advice of Épernon, you have planned to murder all the Catholics in Paris and, as the Faith is dearer to me than my life, I have come to die with the rest.'[2]

'It is a false and malicious slander,' said the King.

'It is devoutly to be hoped so,' said the Duke, 'and that Your Majesty feels the sting of it may increase your understanding of my indignation when I am slandered and calumniated to Your Majesty. I have no desire but loyally to serve you and the Faith and France to the limit of my strength.'

Before Guise's calm assurance, Henri's nerve was failing. The actual physical presence of the Duke precipitated, as it always had since their boyhood, a suspicion of his own inadequacy. He found that he had to raise his voice unnecessarily

'You lie,' he yelled. 'What do you know of loyalty? You are the cause of all the troubles and commotions of France. You lead your precious brothers about like two muzzled bulls whom you will unleash when it suits you to trample down my fairest pastures. You, M. de Guise ...'

In the next room, Laugnac signalled to his men that the moment was upon them. But before the King could finish his sentence, Catherine rose and led him over to the far window. Guise immediately took her place by the Queen's bed and

[2] The Pope, Sixtus V, when told of this reply, wrote: 'The Duke was wrong to make such an answer and we cannot excuse him.' Sixtus, a man of exceedingly humble origin who had found a way to fame by becoming a rabble-rousing Franciscan preacher, was one of the careerist snobs of history and presumably objected to Guise's remark not because it was untrue but because it was discourteous to royalty.

chatted nonchalantly to Louise on family affairs.

'Henri,' said Catherine, 'I begin to fear for your mind.'

'I assure you, Madame, that you have no need. You could say, rather, that I have just come to my senses. It is M. de Guise who is mad to come here without a *garde-du-corps*.'

'If you have not completely lost your wits, you will see that the whole of Paris is his *garde-du-corps*.' And she pointed to the packed, chanting crowds outside the gates.

'But here in the Louvre,' said the King, 'he has no guard.'

'Henri,' said Catherine sharply, 'what exactly you are planning I do not know; but I do know that unless M. de Guise sets foot safely among those out there who are awaiting him, neither your life nor mine will be worth a month's purchase.'

'Why should you think I am planning anything?'

'Am I a fool? Do you think I don't know you? The Swiss! The Scots! Are they a Guard of Honour?' Then, in a flash of insight: 'Where are the Forty-Five?'

Henri, who was convinced of his mother's occult powers, assumed that she must know everything and, in something like panic, said: 'I will give you my word for M. de Guise's safety.'

As they came back from the window, the Duke noticed that Catherine was looking straight at him. He approached Henri and craved permission to retire.

The King immediately granted it, making a rendezvous for the morrow in Catherine's private garden in the Tuileries, where they might discuss more fully all matters pertaining to the safety of the realm.

When Henri heard the deafening acclamations which greeted

Guise when he emerged safely into the street, he said to his mother: 'Can I be King of France as long as he is King of Paris?'

Catherine said: 'I am satisfied that he has no desire but to serve you, my son.'

'Even if you are right,' said the King, 'it is clear that I must waste no time in breaking the spirit of Paris.'

12

The Day of the Barricades

Henri was as good as his word. The meeting with Guise the
following day accomplished nothing. The Duke, to show the
King that he was quite aware of what he had escaped, came
to the Tuileries with a guard of four hundred men, armed.
When he requested that the Cardinal de Bourbon might have
the King's permission to come to Paris, Henri replied blandly:
'Of course, my dear cousin. We all understand the proverb:
"Love me, love my dog!"'

At four in the morning of Thursday 12 May the King
struck. Violating the Parisians' constitutional privilege of
providing their own defences, he introduced 6,000 royal troops,
French and Swiss, into the capital by the Porte St. Honoré.
They were led by Marshal de Biron, Navarre's deputy-
governor for Guienne, a *Politique* who was regarded as a
Huguenot and had acted as adviser to the rebels in the Low
Countries. His presence alone was fuel to the Leaguer fire,
without the provocation of the manner of entry. His troops
marched as if occupying a captured city, with colours flying,
tambours and fifes playing, pikes and halberds at the ready
and the slow matches of the harquebusiers alight. To the
citizens who rushed to their windows in curiosity, the soldiers

shouted: 'See that clean sheets are put on your beds; tonight we shall be sleeping in them with your wives.'

The long procession marched down the Rue St. Honoré and turned off to the Cemetery of the Holy Innocents where Biron gave orders to the various detachments as to which key-points in the city they were to occupy. The Place de Grève in front of the Hôtel de Ville; the Petit-Châtelet, commanding the Petit-Pont; the Pont St. Michel, connecting the Cité with the University quarter on the Left Bank; and Marché-Neuf in the centre of the Cité; the Bastille, whose cannon dominated the Rue St. Antoine, in which was the Hôtel de Guise; and the approaches to the Louvre—all were invested before the people of Paris, momentarily paralysed with rage and astonishment had time to consider counter-measures.

There was, however, one notable oversight. The Place Maubert on the Left Bank, lying between the University and the river, was left unoccupied; and of all the areas of the city this was one of the most inflammable. It was dominated by the Church of Saint-Séverin, whose curé, Jean Prévost, the devoted follower of the Duchess of Montpensier, had exhibited in his cemetery the pictures of the English martyrdoms and who now mounted his pulpit with a cuirass over his cassock to call on all good Frenchmen to fight and die for their Faith and their civil liberties. A tocsin was rung from all the churches in the Quarter. Students from the Sorbonne rushed through the streets crying: 'Alarme! Alarme! Les Huguenots!' The colleges which surrounded the Place Maubert were exhorted by preachers to take up arms in a holy war, and many of the students from the Collège de Fortet and the Collège de Cler-mont did so and paraded in formation shouting: 'Let us fetch the little bugger from the Louvre!' At the request of the *Seize* one of the military leaders of the League, Urban de Laval de

Bois Dauphin,[1] organised the resistance of the Quarter, while another the Comte de Brissac directed the movements of the civilian defenders of Paris as a whole.

The King, considering it important to disclaim any intention of interfering with the municipal privileges of the capital, ordered Marshal de Biron to make an official announcement to the vast crowds which had assembled in the Marché-Neuf to gaze at the five regiments—three Swiss and two French—drawn up there under Crillon. The Marshal therefore assured them, in the King's name, that the only purpose of the introduction of the troops was to expel all foreigners and seditious persons from the capital and that the citizens themselves were still permitted to take up arms, provided they remained within their houses and used them only for the defence of themselves and their families.

Consequently at seven in the morning, Tambonneau, colonel of the city bands, went to the Louvre, craved audience of the King and entreated him to withdraw the professional troops. Henri angrily refused. Hard on the colonel's heels came another deputation, this time from the Parlement. The representatives complained that, in consequence of the unusual introduction of troops into Paris, all business was suspended, the shops were closed and the thoroughfares blocked. They humbly prayed that His Majesty would remedy the evil as quickly as possible. Henri graciously promised to do so, but as the only measure he took was to order Villequier, as Governor of Paris, to perambulate the principal streets with his staff to proclaim the King's pacific intentions and to command the resumption of business, the result was to worsen the situation and to cause Villequier to retreat rapidly into the well-defended Hôtel de Ville.

[1] Five years later he was made a Marshal of France.

Guise, meanwhile, had sent a messenger to Villequier to ask whether the military preparations and the proclamation against 'strangers' were directed specifically against him and his Lorrainers. Villequier had answered with a most emphatic 'Non!' but at the same time had implored the Duke not to exacerbate the situation by appearing in the streets. Guise thereupon sent Pierre de l'Espinac, Archbishop of Lyons, to the Louvre to add his plea for the withdrawal of the soldiers.

'Sire,' said the Archbishop, 'in the present temper of the people, it is like risking your crown on a throw of dice.'

'Monseigneur,' shouted the King, 'I intend to be obeyed and today I will make it plain that I, the King, am master and lord of these rebellious Parisians.'

His face was so contorted with fury that the Archbishop said nothing more and as soon as he was outside the Louvre he went to the house of a friend near-by to borrow a mule so that he could the more quickly reach the Hôtel de Guise to warn the Duke of the King's temper and to assure him that he himself 'was minded to live—or rather as it seemed to him, to die—as his true friend and supporter'.

In the Louvre, Henri's rage became so maniacal and his threats against the denunciation of all the blood and lineage of Lorraine so obscenely bitter that Queen Louise fainted.

In the streets, Crillon realised that, to prevent the ferment in the University quarter spreading until it reached the Louvre, it would be necessary to occupy the Place Maubert. When he tried to do so, he found he was too late. The students superintended by Bois Dauphin and helped by the watermen from the *quais* and the more militant of the crowd had taken it over. Chains were stretched across all the streets leading from the square, which was itself defended by barricades built up with barrels filled with earth, logs and flag-stones torn up from the cloisters and courts of the colleges.[2]

Crillon attempted to retreat but found himself intercepted in the rear by the Comte de Brissac and an armed body of citizens and Leaguers from the Faubourg Saint Germain. More barricades were built up along the streets at intervals of thirty paces; the women brought out the furniture of their houses to aid in the construction and Crillon soon found himself unable to advance or retreat and his communications with Biron cut off.

The example of the students' barricades was taken up from street to street. On occasions, good-natured Swiss helped exhausted citizens to carry loads of cobblestones or heave heavy barrels upright. They had been assured that His Majesty's purpose was, strictly, to defend Paris against foreigners. They had not seen any foreigners and they approved of the citizens' efforts to help themselves. It seemed only right to encourage them.

By nine o'clock in the morning the streets were completely fortified, the barricades being defended not only by men armed with muskets, swords and clubs but by women at the upper windows prepared to hurl stones, tiles and blinding torrents of sand on any attackers below.

'These barricades,' wrote an observer, 'were solid, strong and impassable. It has been calculated that if the citizens had left the doors of their houses open, 100,000 men could not have taken the city, defended and barricaded as it then was.' And Bernadino de Mendoza, the Spanish Ambassador, wrote to King Philip: 'The strength of the defences is amazing. The

[2] As one historian has put it, 'Crillon beheld the rise as if by magic of the first barricade which ushered in that mode of street-fighting which since has been an especial favourite of the Parisian populace.'

city of Paris has concentrated for the occasion the spirit and energy of two hundred towns.'

He added a post-script which suddenly wrenched a local improvisation into an international perspective: 'It is certain that the King of France will have his hands so tied before the Armada sails that it will be impossible for him even in words, let alone in deeds, to help the Queen of England.'

Guise made a last attempt to calm the storm by persuading the Papal Nuncio to visit the King and urge him 'not to ruin the most beautiful city in the world and cause much innocent blood to be shed'. Henri took as little notice of him as he had of previous visitors and the Nuncio, after leaving him, went in despair to the Queen-Mother.

Catherine's answer surprised him. 'I have nothing but praise for the advice you have given my son,' she said, 'and I would myself urge it on him were it not that I have resolved not to speak to him on the subject.' At the Nuncio's look of incredulity, she explained: 'You ought to know that the King's plans have been made without my knowledge or any consultation with me and I will confess to you that I am greatly hurt by this evidence of my son's lack of trust in me.'

Whatever her private feelings, Catherine realised that no one but herself could resolve the public tumult. Henri, faced with the unforeseen possibility of the piecemeal destruction of the Royal troops, could think of nothing but sending to his 'gallant son', Épernon, at Rouen an order to advance immediately on Paris with all the men he could muster. To avoid this final disaster the Queen-Mother determined to act on her own responsibility.

When Biron next came to the Louvre, about midday, to

report the position she insisted on seeing him. He informed her that the Swiss were everywhere laying down their arms. 'In truth, Madame,' he said, 'they have no alternative to save their lives; they are so enclosed and hemmed in by the barricades that it is impossible for any of the King's regiments to extricate themselves unless they could burrow underground like mice.'

'Then, M. le Maréchal,' said Catherine, decisively, 'you will go to the Hôtel de Guise and command the Duke in the King's name to suppress the tumult and deliver His Majesty's troops.'

When Biron delivered the message, Guise said. 'It was not my wish to have any part in these proceedings. As His Majesty requested me, I have not left my Hôtel, although many have asked me to. This unrest has nothing to do with me, though I am not unaware that many will endeavour to make it appear so. It is the result of the foolish counsels to which the King listens. Let his councillors undo the evil they have done.'

'Monseigneur,' said the Marshal, 'in the opinion of Her Majesty the Queen-Mother, there is no one but yourself who can do this service to the Crown and she is trusting to your—'

'Loyalty?' There was an ironic undertone to his interruption.

'No, M. le Duc, your magnaminity.'

When Guise, dressed in his white satin doublet and with nothing but a riding-switch in his hand, leaving even his sword to be carried by his page, appeared in the street outside his Hôtel, the shouts of acclamation were, if possible, even more deafening than those that had greeted his arrival in Paris. A passage was immediately opened for him and, accompanied by Biron, he went with him first to the Hôtel de Ville. In front of it, on the Place de Grève, the Swiss were on their knees, disarmed, and in considerable peril from attacks by the armed citizens.

Guise held up his hand for silence and—according to a Huguenot spectator—'the fury of this imbecile populace was hushed at the mere sound of his voice, so besotted were they by the love of him'. The Duke, addressing the people, asked that, since God had been so merciful to them on this day, 'resplendent with Divine protection', as to give them and their families liberty, they in gratitude would allow the Swiss to depart unharmed. The people roared assent and the astonished soldiers, who joined in the cheers, were permitted to rise and march through the barricades to the Louvre.

Guise then proceeded to rescue other portions of the beleaguered troops. At the Marché-Neuf, they were in worse plight than at the Place de Grève. Here, unfortunately, the Swiss harquebusiers had refused to extinguish their matches; a piece had gone off by accident and a citizen had been killed. Immediately they were assailed by a volley of shots from the roofs and windows of the surrounding houses and more than sixty were dead or wounded. The remainder had discarded their arms, fallen on their knees and waving their rosaries cried: *'Bonne France! Bon Catholique!'*. The firing thereupon ceased, but the situation remained tense. When Guise and Biron arrived, many were still lying in their blood with their wounds untended, others were imploring mercy.

'Those who have caused this misery,' said Guise, 'ought to be made to compensate for it.'

'True, Monseigneur,' Biron replied, 'evil be on the head of whoever counselled it. It is true that I brought the Swiss here, but in doing so I was only obeying the King.'

Once more Guise made his appeal to the citizens, who immediately started to care for the wounded and to make way for the Swiss to return to the Louvre.

So the Duke and the Marshal went from point to point until all the troops were freed. Passing an enormous barricade at the entrance to the Pont St. Michel, Guise congratulated the citizens who had constructed it with: '*Mes amis*, you have shown marvellous skill and valour!'

'Monseigneur,' the leader replied, 'we were as feeble as flies before you came; it is your presence that has made us as brave as lions to defend our Faith and our freedom.'

The situation was completely restored by five o'clock in the afternoon when Catherine went officially to the Hôtel de Guise to express her gratitude to the Duke. Having heard of her intention, he was waiting at the gate to receive her and to hand her out of her chair. They spoke openly in the courtyard so that their attendants and some onlookers could hear them plainly and, as if by some tacit understanding, they immediately agreed that all blame for the day's misfortunes must be laid on the folly of the King's advisers.

Guise summed the matter up with: 'Madame, the wit of all of us combined can hardly remedy what has been so unhappily done today. The good people of Paris have never before been coerced by a garrison and they will never submit to it. Moreover, they believe that His Majesty, your son, intends to take the lives of many of his Catholic subjects, mine in particular. Nevertheless, I have done all in my power to allay the tumult and to reassure the citizens.'

Catherine replied that it was never the King's intention to infringe the rights of the citizens and that he had only wished to purge Paris of certain turbulent foreigners who were bent on stirring up trouble.

'Of that, Madame, you must realise that I know nothing. I was not aware of any foreigners, nor had I any part in promoting the insurrection, as everyone can bear witness.'

The cheers from some of the bystanders prompted Catherine to suggest that it would be better to continue their conversation indoors.

Once in the privacy of Guise's room, her demeanour completely changed. In a harsh voice she announced: 'M. de Guise, my son and I intend to hold you responsible for any further disturbances in the city. You will command the people to lay down their arms and dismantle the barricades immediately.'

'If I had the authority to do so—'

'I have told you: it is His Majesty's wish.'

'Naturally I do not doubt Your Majesty, but a private word is hardly sufficient in so public a matter. If the King designs to appoint me his Lieutenant-General, I shall be happy to exercise responsibility.'

'What else do you want?'

'For myself, Madame, nothing whatever. I do not even want the Lieutenant-Generalship, but I can see no other way to serve His Majesty as I would wish to.'

'Suppose I should say, M. de Guise, that the cause of all this is your disobedience in coming to Paris when the King had forbidden it and that, however innocent you may try to make your conduct appear, your real intention is to gain control of the King for your own ends? Suppose I should say this, what would your answer be?'

'I should say to you, Madame, that, as far as I understand it, you yourself were not averse to my return to Paris and that, since I had committed no crime, no one had any right to prevent it. When the King asked me on Tuesday whether I had any soldiers in Paris, I answered him truly that I had not a single man within fifty leagues of the city. This morning, when the Royal troops were being posted, I was asleep in bed not so much dreaming of any disturbance. As for gaining control of the King, let us be honest, Madame. You know that, had I wished it, I could have taken him prisoner a dozen times today, since the only limit on my power, because of the good people of Paris, has been my determination to act rightly out of the fear and the love of God.'

'Those are fine phrases, but do you wish me to believe that you have no purposes of your own?'

'I have already told you, Madame, that I desire nothing whatever for myself. My one wish is to serve the Crown.'

'Then, M. de Guise, will you accompany me back to the Louvre to assure the King in person of your loyalty.'

'No, Madame.'

'Why not?'

'Your memory is surely not so short as to have forgotten our visit there on Monday?'

'I can assure you that, today, the King has nothing but good-will towards you.'

Guise understood perfectly that, in the changed circumstances, Catherine's only care was her son. The Duke was still grateful to her for having helped, from whatever motive, to save his life from Henri's assassins, but he doubted whether, should he be foolish enough to go to the Louvre with her now, she would do so again. Also, he had suddenly found her lying tedious.

'Your Majesty,' he said, 'I must be frank with you. My most trusted friends advise me not to enter the Louvre and put my life at the mercy of my enemies. They know, as I do, that the King wishes to destroy certain people, including myself, because he hates everyone who opposes Épernon. Also your son still secretly supports the claims of Henry of Navarre to be his heir. He has not fulfilled the promises he made in the treaty which you and I, Madame, negotiated. Therefore I shall not advise the people of Paris to lay down their arms until His Majesty has shown that he intends to keep his word.'

'In what way?'

'By proclaiming that the *soi-disant* King of Navarre is incapable of succeeding him and by summoning a States-General to settle the succession; by banishing the *mignon* Épernon from court and depriving him of his honours and dignities; by desposing the *mignon* Villequier from the Governorship of Paris; and by dismissing the idle gang of ruffians who are known as the *Forty-Five*; by—'

'M. le Duc,' Catherine interrupted, 'what will the people of France think or the princes of Europe believe, if the King should make such craven concessions? Would they not say that, whatever may appear, you have taken the Crown from his head?'

'Madame, no one but you and I would know that it was not a free concession from his own wisdom. Nor, in any case, is it shameful in a king to keep his word.'

Catherine continued to argue angrily, but Guise was immovable. His last word was: 'Now that the King, Madame, has at last plainly revealed his hostile intentions against the League and his hatred of me, I have resolved either to die or to make the Faith secure in France by whatever means I can.'

When the King was told these things by his mother on her return to the Louvre, he sat silent for hours 'like the image of a dead man'. Then he started to cry and mutter: 'Betrayed! Betrayed! So many treacheries!'

Eventually he resolved to leave Paris next day. He closeted himself with Villequier and Bellièvre, who had been with him on the memorable occasion, fourteen years ago, when he had managed to escape from Poland to return to claim the crown of France.[3] His mood brightened with the reminiscences.

'Paris should be child's play compared with Cracow,' he said.

'Except,' said Villequier, 'that all the gates are guarded by Brissac's men.'

'You are certain of that, Réné?'

'I have made an official inspection. No one is able to leave the city without a special pass signed by one of the *Seize*.'

The King turned to Bellièvre, who on the earlier escape had nearly wrecked everything by trying to insist on diplomatically correct procedure: 'What does protocol suggest, my friend?'

'Your Majesty is pleased to jest at my mistakes.'

'Not in the least. I only wished to be assured that you did not advise me to ask permission of M. de Guise as King of Paris.'

'There must be some way—'

The King took a key from his pocket. 'It is here,' he said. 'There is one gate they have forgotten.'

'But I assure you, sire, I visited them all myself.'

'This one they would not count.'

It was the key of the little private postern of the Queen-Mother's new garden of the Tuileries which actually lay partly outside the walls.

Just after Midday on Friday, 14 May, the King accompanied by Villequier, Bellièvre, the Abbé del Bene and a sprinkling of courtiers, sauntered unhurriedly from the Louvre, followed by a pack of Henri's diminutive dogs, to take exercise in the Tuileries gardens. Once within the protecting wall, they

[3] See *The Last of the Valois*, Chapter 6.

crossed quickly to the stables, picked what horses were available and rode pell-mell on the road to Chartres.

At Chaîllot the King paused to look back at the capital and curse it. With a great oath he swore that he would return only as a conqueror through a breach his cannon had made in the walls.

He could not guess that he would never return.

13

Government by Dissimulation

The escape from Paris, accentuated by memories of his flight from Poland, had a rejuvenating effect on the King. For a moment, the amused adventurer, warily reducing odds by his courage and his cunning, replaced the satiated monarch, trying to escape the boredom of too much knowledge by retreating into trivialities.

One thing above all was clear to him: Guise must die. As long as he lived, the League and Lorraine, not the Valois, would in fact rule France. Henri's personal hatred of the Duke, which had been born in their early twenties when he discovered that Guise was Margot's lover and had hardened murderously when Guise had caused the death of the beloved Quélus, now took on the appearance of a public duty. He blamed himself that he had allowed him to escape on Monday afternoon when all preparations had been so carefully made for his assassination. The ease of Henri's own escape to Chartres had made him think that he had overestimated the danger from the Parisians had Guise never emerged alive from the Louvre. In part he blamed his mother for her decisive advice and almost allowed himself unworthy doubts of her real intentions. She had acted throughout as Guise's guardian. Was she also prepared to be his ally in return for his support of her grandson, Henry of Lorraine, as the next King of France? At the very least, Henri decided, she might be, in her seventieth year, losing her judgment.

He was, however, honest enough to dismiss the thought as soon as he entertained it. What he was trying to formulate, he realised, was a method of circumventing his mother's policies so that he could plan Guise's murder—of which she would certainly disapprove—without her interference. But she had a way of always discovering his plans.

Following this train of thought, he suddenly stumbled on the obvious. Retz, Nevers, Bellièvre, Cheverny, his Chancellor, and Villeroi, his Secretary of State, even, in the first instance, Villequier had all been chosen for him by her. They naturally advised him as she desired and loyally reported to her his intentions. Her hatred of Épernon was fundamentally due to the fact that the favourite's fidelity was entirely to him.

With great clarity, the King saw what he must do. All these advisers must be dismissed and replaced by competent men whose first loyalty was to him. In the case of Épernon, it was unfortunately necessary that, in the present state of the country, Henri would have to appear to sacrifice him, at least temporarily. But, with a little care, a virtue might be made of that necessity. He could be sent to Angoulême, of which he was Governor. There, within easy reach of La Rochelle on the one hand and Guienne on the other, he could in a crisis summon Huguenot help and, in any case, could open secret conversations with Navarre. To counter Guise, the King was now prepared to come to terms with Navarre and to ensure his succession whether or not he returned to the Church.

In his relations with Guise himself, Henri determined to

show the utmost amiability. The Duke must be lulled into security. He should be made Lieutenant-General of the Kingdom as a public acknowledgement that he was the greatest man in France. He should also be confirmed as Grand Master of the Household, ostensibly as a gesture of private good-will, actually as a guarantee of his official presence in whichever royal residence Henri happened to be occupying at whatever time was decided for his assassination.

The degree of dissimulation this policy would entail was itself a challenge to Henri's power of acting and the practice of it gave him some relief from his overmastering boredom and frustration. His mother had often inculcated the maxim: *'Reculez pour mieux sauter'*. Now he would give a practical demonstration of it which would instruct his instructress.

Miron found him still occasionally talking to himself. He was repeating 'Mon cousin de Guise' with every variety of inflection from affectionate greeting to ironic dismissal.

The flight of the King from Paris was a severe blow to Guise, in that it left him no alternative to appearing as Henri wished to represent him—a rebellious subject who had taken up arms against the Crown. He issued an immediate manifesto deploring that 'it had not pleased the King to witness a little longer my respect and filial obedience' and further announcing: 'I have taken the Bastille, the Arsenal and other strong places into my hands; I have caused the coffers of the Treasury to be sealed, in order that I may transmit them into the hands of His Majesty when he is in a pacific mood such as we hope to render him by our prayers to God, by the intercession of His Holiness the Pope and of all Christian Princes; or, if the evil continues, I hope by the same means to preserve the Faith and the

Catholics and to free them from the persecution which the confederates of the heretics about the King are preparing.'

Catherine, meanwhile, remained in Paris as the King's representative, continuing to negotiate with Guise and receiving her old friend the Cardinal de Bourbon, who arrived in the capital in lay dress, attended by fifty archers, splendid in his colours of crimson and gold, and took up his residence, as Heir Apparent, in the Hôtel de Guise.

By Saturday, May 14, all the barricades had been dismantled and order had been completely restored.

There were still those in Paris who remained affectionately loyal to the King. They were the religious confraternities whom Henri had patronised—the Penitents of Notre Dame, which he had founded, and the White Flagellants, of which, since the first year of his reign, he had been the patron.[1] They decided to make a pilgrimage to Chartres and requested Joyeuse's brother, who had become 'le Père Ange' of the Capuchins to lead it. He consented and a grotesque procession set out from Paris representing the scene on the Via Dolorosa to make the point 'that as Christ pardoned the enemies who had scourged and ill-treated Him so the King was bound to forgive the Parisians the outrage to which he had been subjected'. Joyeuse impersonated Christ and the Cross was of cardboard.

A spectator described the scene: 'First walked a man with a long beard, dirty and uncombed, blowing occasional blasts on a cracked trumpet. Then came three other men of ferocious aspect, each having a copper basin on his head instead of a Roman helmet, and wearing over his sackcloth a rusty suit of armour. These persons dragged after them le Père Ange,

[1] See *The Last of the Valois*, p. 113.

bound hand and foot, and clad in a white vestment in shape like an alb. On his head was a wig and upon this a crown of thorns was placed, while drops of blood made by red paint bespattered his face. He carried a large cross beneath the pretended weight of which he frequently feigned to stumble and fall. Behind le Père Ange walked four men, also wearing armour, holding the ropes with which he was bound, who at intervals lashed furiously with a scourge upon the cords. On each side of le Père Ange walked two young Capuchin monks, impersonating one the Virgin Mary, the other Mary Magdalene. Their arms were crossed on their breasts, their tearful eyes were raised to Heaven and they prostrated themselves each time le Père Ange fell to the ground.'

Following this *piéce de resistance* came a procession, several hundred strong, of Capuchins, Penitents and Flagellants with a sprinkling of lay Parisians. They arrived in Chartres— it was Tuesday 17 May—in the late afternoon, when the King was hearing vespers. They poured into the Cathedral, beating their breasts and crying: 'Miséricorde! Miséricorde!' and fell prostrate over one another before the High Altar.

The start of the procession from Paris had been watched by Guise with considerable distaste. The reception of it in Chartres was received by the King with even more. The idea that it would please him made him, in his new mood, irrationally angry. He gave an abrupt order that the shrieks and moans of the Penitents should immediately cease and, looking through rather than at le Père Ange, said to him: 'I deplore from the bottom of my heart your credulity, M. de Joyeuse, that you should be so misled by my monks as to lend yourself to this ludicrous exhibition.'

Crillon came forward and offered the King the services of

his guard to give the Penitents each a dozen stripes as an exhibition of how it should have been done. Henri, however, spared them this lesson and confined himself to refusing to speak further to any of them and leaving the cathedral immediately.

Next day, however, he condescended to send a message to the Parlement of Paris that it was his intention to take measures to provide a Catholic successor to the throne of France selected from among the princes of the blood royal. The Cardinal de Bourbon thereupon announced that, as his only demand was that the sceptre of St. Louis should not be desecrated by the grasp of a heretic, he would await the outcome without making any further political intervention and left the Hôtel de Guise to return, in suitable ecclesiastical dress, to his Abbey of Saint-Germain.

One of the Cardinal's nephews, a Bourbon Prince of the Blood, to whom the King's announcement gave considerable food for thought was Charles Count of Soissons, Condé's twenty-one-year-old half-brother. Soissons had remained a Catholic, but he had joined Navarre just before the battle of Coutras because, on the one hand, he had realised that he had nothing to hope from King Henri, and, on the other, that he had fallen in love with Navarre's sister, Catherine. After Coutras, where Soissons commanded the Huguenot right wing, the young Count had returned with Navarre to Pau and become betrothed to Catherine. Navarre, however, who regarded his sister as a good bargaining asset as long as she remained unmarried (he had confessed to one of his friends: 'I have offered my sister to half the princes of Europe, but I don't mean any of them to have her') delayed the wedding as long as he possibly could. To Soisson's demands for an immediate marriage Navarre insisted that there was no hurry. The cousins quarrelled incessantly until Soissons threatened to withdraw from the Huguenot alliance. At the beginning of the year, however, Condé died suddenly and mysteriously. His second wife was generally believed to have poisoned him and the legal formalities that followed—including the questioning and torture of some of the minor servants of Condé's household—gave Navarre a genuine excuse for postponing the Soissons marriage. By the Day of the Barricades no wedding preparations had even begun.

The news from Paris reached Navarre and Soissons while they were making a military progress in Poitou. It brought Soisson's irritation to a climax. The opportunity of the Catholic Princes of the Blood, he thought, had at last arrived and he could not sufficiently regret that he had not been on the spot to take advantage of it. When Navarre suggested that, in a time of such uncertainty, it would be advisable for them to retire to La Rochelle, Soissons lost his temper and angrily told his cousin that he could go where he liked but, as far as he personally was concerned, he was going to Chartres to throw himself humbly at Henri's feet and implore his pardon for having fought against Joyeuse at Coutras.

Navarre had his own problems. Since he had discovered that the *reiters* had intended to kidnap him and take him forcibly back to Germany as a hostage for the vast sums owed to John Casimir by the French Huguenots, his enthusiasm for the Protestant cause, as such, had appreciably waned. He would gladly have abandoned it had it not appeared to be his only way of gaining power. As it was, the best he could do was to make tentative overtures to the King.

To minimize the effects of his excommunication, he had approached the Sorbonne and the Parlement of Paris and requested the setting-up of a Council of theologians to instruct him in Catholicism. At the same time he had asked that the question of succession should be referred to the States-General. This resulted in the leader of the *Politiques* declaring: 'If consideration for public weal and for religion has made many men the followers of Guise, so also the declaration of the King of Navarre that he will change his faith in deference to a council and his condition in accordance with the decrees of the States-General, has led a number of good Catholics and true Frenchmen to the view that what is at issue is not a question of religion but of politics. If the Catholics join Navarre they will certainly bring him back to the Church.'

To the irritated and suspicious Huguenots, Navarre had to explain that he had no intention whatever of changing his religion and that his apparent complaisance in the matter was merely diplomatic necessity. Dissimulation was imperative. His co-religionists, however, were by no means convinced and he was forced to call a General Assembly of the Huguenots at La Rochelle, which set up a Council of Twelve, consisting of elected Calvinist deputies, whose advice in religious matters Navarre bound himself to follow.

Another reason for strained relations between him and his stricter followers was his continuing amours, which he conducted with less and less discretion. At La Rochelle he was openly living with the girl whose seduction had occasioned his public confession on the field of Coutras. She had borne him a child of whose death he informed Corisande, seeking sympathy: 'I am greatly distressed by the death of my little son, who was just beginning to talk.' Corisande was less sympathetic than she might have been. She did indeed write to him but in a note which provoked the reply: 'I have received your letter. It required very little time to read it. Do you think it right to behave so strangely?' She had, however, discovered that he was at the same time paying court to another lady whom he had promised (in writing) to marry as soon as he could divorce Margot, and Corisande reproached him for his fickleness. He replied: 'My life! I am sorely displeased when I find you entertain doubts of me. Spitefully, I will not endeavour to remove them. You are greatly at fault, for I swear to you that I never loved you more ardently than I do at this moment and I would sooner die than break the promises I have made to you. Believe this, and live in confidence of my fidelity. Good-night, my Life! A million kisses.'[2]

Altogether, both personally and politically, Navarre was coming profoundly to resent the position of Huguenot leader which circumstances had thrust upon him. He, no less than Soissons, wanted to make his peace with Henri and, as soon as his cousin had left him, he sent a secret messenger to Chartres to discover whether Henri would accept his offer of himself and the Huguenot army.

Henri allowed it to be understood that in principle he would welcome any help against Guise but that it was impossible to make any certain plans until the outcome of 'the Enterprise of England' was known. 'If the Spanish fleet is defeated,' he said, 'all good things will follow.'

By Midsummer Day, it seemed that the Armada would

[2] On this letter one of Navarre's biographers comments: 'He was being perfectly honest, because he never considered that going to bed with one woman had the least effect on his feelings for another, and it troubled him when those he loved could not see eye to eye with him.'

certainly fail. On that June 24 Medina Sidonia had to write to King Philip that the winds and the sea and the weather and an unexpected gale had shattered the fleet. Several ships had lost sails and spars, many had sprung a leak and he had been forced to run for the shelter of Corunna, accompanied by the ships that lay nearest to him, though others had been driven before the storm into the open sea.

The Admiral feared that the disaster would soon be known in England and that English ships and Huguenot pirates from La Rochelle would hunt down the distressed vessels which had not managed to make some sheltering port. The weather, he said still was more like December than June. There was much sickness among the soldiers and sailors and so great a proportion of the provisions taken aboard at Lisbon had proved worthless that there were supplies for only a short campaign.

If the reports from England were reliable, the reluctant Admiral insisted, he would face a greatly superior force; and in any case the Armada could not continue its voyage until the ships had been repaired and reprovisioned and reinforcements collected. Meanwhile there would be grave danger to the trade with the Indies and to the King's dominions, for his enemies, and especially the rebels in Flanders, would take fresh courage at the news of this mishap to the fleet. Medina Sidonia predicted that Parma would not be able to muster the required invasion force, even if the Armada reached the Channel. He therefore ventured to suggest that the enterprise should be considered to have miscarried and should therefore be abandoned and that the King should endeavour to make peace with England on honourable terms.

On July 1 the King signed the Edict of Union which conceded

to the League all the points Guise had discussed with the Queen-Mother in Paris and a solemn *Te Deum* to celebrate the peace was sung in Notre Dame without the presence of the King. The one thing Henri would not do was to return to the capital. Such a step, he considered, would be construed as a gesture of forgiveness to the Parisians. He would re-enter the faithless city, as he had sworn, through a breach in the walls made by his cannon or not at all.

Catherine reproached him for it. 'Alas, my son,' she said, 'is it possible that you have grown so unforgiving? Your disposition seems to have changed completely.'

'I think it has, mother,' he replied in mock sorrow. 'But what can I do about it? That wicked Épernon who, they all say, did me so much harm, must have changed it. But who knows? Now he is safe in Angoulême, I may become myself again.'

Such irony had now become habitual with him and it disconcerted others beside Catherine. When Guise came to Chartres for a public reconciliation, Henri's reception of him was embarrassing in its display of affection. When the Duke knelt to kiss the royal hand, the King raised him immediately and embraced him as effusively as if he had been Épernon. At the great banquet which followed, the King asked: 'Whom shall we pledge?'

'It is Your Majesty to choose,' said Guise.

'Then, cousin,' said Henri, 'let us drink to our good friends the Huguenots.'

'Very well, sire.'

'And, of course,' the King added quickly, 'to our good Barricaders of Paris. We must not forget them, must we?'

Guise drank the toast smiling, though he was anything but amused. After the banquet was over, he wrote to the Spanish

Ambassador: 'It is not easy to judge the state of affairs here. If we might go by appearances, we should apprehend a great change for the better; but we have not yet had time to judge whether it is a marvellous mutation and, as it were, a new world or whether it is an extraordinary dissimulation—one greater than a French mind can carry out.'

In this art, the half-Italian Henri had obviously the advantage, but Guise was not far behind him and *'L'agréable dissimulation du Duc de Guise'* became one of the catchwords of the Court.

The sudden arrival of the Spanish Ambassador a few days later resuscitated political acrimony at Chartres. Mendoza came to announce that the Spanish fleet had won a great victory over the English in the Channel and that the Spaniards had landed on English soil. The Ambassador went straight to the Bishop's Palace where the King was staying and to the courtiers who were awaiting the King's appearance he exclaimed: *'Victoria! Victoria! vive el rey Catolico!'*

When Henri, accompanied by Guise, entered the presence-chamber, Mendoza retailed his news to the Duke's obvious delight. The King, however, replied drily that the Ambassador must be labouring under some unhappy delusion, as he had that morning received a despatch from M. de Gourdan, Governor of Calais, informing him that, on the contrary, the English had thoroughly defeated the Armada, destroying a dozen ships and killing 5,000 men. Moreover, one of the largest ships was lying a complete wreck on the Calais sands while the rest had been scattered by a violent gale. Mendoza withdrew in confusion and the *Te Deum* for which he had originally asked was not sung.

Guise and Henri both decided to discuss the matter, for the moment, lightly and not to exacerbate each other's feelings. But Henri was generally credited with the inspiration, if not with the actual authorship, of the placard which appeared all over Paris: 'If anyone knows the whereabouts of the Armada of Spain, victorious over England, and will tell the Spanish Ambassador, he will give him five francs reward.' And Guise organised the Turkish galley-slaves from the wrecked galleon at Calais, who claimed freedom as a result of landing on French soil, to make their petition to Henri on his way to Mass. There were three hundred of them lining his way 'all being nude as they were when they held the oar'.

14

The States-General at Blois

During the last week of September the representatives of the nation started to assemble at Blois where the King was to open the States-General on October 16. The deputies of the *Clergy*, numbering 134, met for their private deliberations in the hall of the Dominican convent under the chairmanship of their elected spokesman, the Cardinal of Guise; the 104 *Noblesse*, under the Comte de Brissac, of barricade fame, in the Palais de Justice; and the Third Estate, the *Tiers*, numbering 190, mostly lawyers and municipal officials, under la Chapelle Marteau, one of the most fiery of the *Seize*, in the Hôtel de Ville. The composition and the leadership of the Three Estates left no doubt that the assembly was *Guisard* to the core and its concern for religion was emphasised by a proclamation of a three-day fast, followed by a public profession of Catholicism and a Mass, celebrated by the Cardinal de Bourbon, at which everyone communicated. The preponderance of deputies with Leaguer sympathies was itself a minor defeat for the King, for, as Guise had written to Mendoza (who had temporarily returned to Spain): 'Everywhere in France they are trying to arrange the election of deputies who favour the Princes of the Blood and want, under the pretext of lessening taxes, peace with the Huguenots. I have left nothing undone on my side, but have sent into all the provinces and bailiwicks men whom I can trust to work against their efforts.'

Before the meeting of the Estates, Henri had carried out the palace revolution he had planned. Without any warning, he had delivered simultaneously to eight of his closest counsellors an identical note written in his own hand: 'I am very well satisfied with your services but go immediately to your house and stay there until I send for you. Do not ask the reason for this note, but obey me.' The dismissed men were replaced by nonentities of unimpeachable integrity and little ability. The new Chancellor, indeed, when he came to Chartres to ask permission to refuse the honour, was obliged to ask which of the three persons in the room in which he was received was the King.

Catherine was furious. The Venetian Ambassador reported: 'She resents this action of the King her son the more because most of those dismissed were appointed to serve by her during her regencies, and seeing thing of such importance done without her knowing anything about it, she is entirely beside herself.'

But all she said to Henri was: 'You have made great changes?' to be met with: 'Yes, Cheverny was a swindling rogue, Bellièvre was a Huguenot, Villeroi an ambitious braggart who wanted to keep everything in his own hands, Brulart completely worthless and Pinart an avaricious scoundrel who would sell his own father and mother.' And, to make it plain that he had no intention of allowing his mother to interfere further with his plans, he told her that he had given strict orders that the new men were to employ no one who had served under their predecessors.

The Court noticed that none of the new ministers went near the Queen-Mother, and Henri, in a fit of combined conscience and caution, decided to make an *amende* when he opened the States-General. 'I cannot pass over in silence,' he said in the Speech from the Throne, 'the infinite pains which the Queen my mother has taken to meet the evils which afflict the State and I think it right to render to her in this illustrious assembly, in my own name and in the name of the nation, public thanks. Not only is it true that I owe her the honour of being your master seated on the leading throne of Christendom, but if I have any experience, if I have been educated in good principles, whatever piety may be seen in me, above all the zeal I have for the establishment of the Catholic faith and the reformation of the State—I owe them all to her.

'What work has she not undertaken to appease the troubles that have arisen and to establish everywhere the true worship of God and public peace? Has her advanced age been able to induce her to spare herself? Has she not for this cause sacrificed her health? It is indeed from her that I have learnt to find all my pleasure in the cares that are inseparable from government. That is why I have convoked this States-General of the realm as the surest and most salutary remedy for the evil by which my people are afflicted and it was my mother who confirmed me in that resolution.'

Catherine sitting at his right hand listened with no visible emotion to this encomium, though she smiled an answer to Henri's bow to her. The opening *séance royale* of the States-General was held in the Great Hall of the Château de Blois where a large stage, with three steps, had been placed between the third and fourth pillar of the immense room. On it was a daïs with the King's throne and footstool between two smaller Chairs of State, covered with violet velvet spangled with gold *fleur-de-lys*, for the two Queens. In front of the King on the lowest step was the tabouret—a stool with arms but no back—on which Guise, in his capacity of Grand Master of the Royal Household, sat facing the assembled deputies with his back to the King. During the opening Speech from the Throne, men's eyes were on him rather than on Henri. Everyone realised that the oration, brilliantly delivered with soft plausibility and biting innuendoes, was a declaration of war.

The King, having paid tribute to his mother, vindicated his policy, admitting, with an air of humility, that he was not altogether blameless: '*Peccavi*, gentlemen, I have sinned. I admit it freely. But I will amend my ways. I have already started to put my household in order and I promise you that in future where there were two capons, there will be only one.' As regards religion, he avowed his resolve to die for the Catholic faith if necessary and in a notable figure of speech said that he claimed no mausoleum more superb and honourable than one reared on the ruins of heresy. He would see to it that no heretic should ever succeed to the throne of France. He solemnly accepted the Edict of Union and, for its better confirmation, invited the deputies to be present on the following Tuesday when all might again swear to observe it and he himself would once more recognise it as a fundamental law of the monarchy.

'God is my witness,' he continued, 'how freely I have convoked this assembly. I have not intrigued against the liberty of the deputies. I have not tried to bribe or corrupt the electors. Had I done so, I should blush for my conduct, as those should blush who have resorted to such unworthy means, if there be any such before me now.'

Guise remained impassive. This, after all, was predictable politics and no one, he thought, was ingenuous enough to expect truth from Henri. But, as the King continued and the Duke realised his intention, the assembly noticed a flush of anger on Guise's cheek.

'I have already confessed,' said Henri, 'that I have transgressed by being too negligent in certain matters, but you must not imagine that I alone am responsible for the afflictions of the country. Some of the greatest princes of my realm have entered into unlawful leagues and associations. With my usual clemency, I am prepared to overlook the past. Do not forget that such leagues cannot be tolerated under my authority and are formally contrary to it. All leagues, associations, practices, schemes, intelligences, raising of men or money or acceptance of the same, within or without the kingdom, are acts pertaining to the King alone and, without his permission, are crimes of *lèse-majesté* if committed by a subject.

'I have said I am content to forgive the past, but I declare here and now for the future, after the conclusion of this States-General when the laws made here shall be ratified, any of my subjects who do not abandon such leagues or who participate in them without my permission shall be attainted and convicted of the crime of *lèse-majesté*.'

As soon as the assembly was dismissed, Guise hurried to the apartment of the Cardinal de Bourbon, who had been suddenly taken ill and had consequently been absent from the proceedings. The Duke told him of the King's speech, with its accusations of disloyalty and its threat to outlaw the League, and asked the Cardinal's advice as to what course should now be followed. The Cardinal, who had not quite grasped the extent of recent changes, gave his accustomed reply: 'Consult the Queen-Mother!'

Catherine, however, had nothing to suggest. 'You must be aware, M. de Guise, how far I am from having the influence with which my son credited me in his speech. As he misled the deputies in that so he may also have done in your matter.'

'You can say no more than that, Madame?'

Catherine gave him one of the half-smiles which he knew how to interpret. 'Is the speech printed yet?' she said.

Guise then went to see his brother, the Cardinal of Guise who, with Pierre l'Espinac, Archbishop of Lyons, was staying not with the others at the castle but, in order to escape espionage and preserve their freedom of movement, in the Hôtel d'Alluye in the town.

He found the Comte de Brissac and La Chapelle Marteau already there, exasperated to the last degree by the King's speech which, they said, branded the clergy, the Catholic nobility and the municipality of Paris as traitors.

'He has always tried to do this,' said Guise. 'It is a consequence of his own treachery to the Faith. Because Philip of Spain supports the League, I am branded as a traitor who would sell my country to Spain. No one who knows me would believe it, but he must use it to palliate his own greater treachery in selling France to the *reiters* and the Huguenots.'

'The question of the moment, my dear brother,' said the Cardinal, 'is how to prevent the good-hearted fools who do not know you believing it.'

'There is only one way, Louis, and that is by preventing their knowing about it. The speech is not yet printed.'

'It will be by tomorrow,' said Brissac, 'and in any case the

King is not likely to change it. I understand a copy was sent to the printers in Paris yesterday.'

'The King must be persuaded to omit that part beginning "some of the greatest princes of my realm",' said the Archbishop of Lyons.

'It will be difficult to move him in this mood, but it is possible that Your Grace's own eloquence might prevail with him.'

'I will seek an audience immediately,' said the Archbishop.

'And I,' said La Chapelle Marteau, 'in case you should fail, will give the royal printers instruction to print nothing until the *Seize* authorises it.'

The Archbishop, as soon as the King received him, went straight to the point and demanded the erasure of the offending passages. 'They reflect grossly on the loyalty of Your Majesty's faithful servants and though we are content to become in the Assembly itself the butt of Your Majesty's sarcasm, we cannot allow such comments on our conduct to go forth in print to the whole realm, which may misconstrue them.'

'I spoke, Your Grace, as it was my duty to speak and if anything more is said on the subject I shall think that treasonable violence is intended.'

'Your Majesty is free to think whatever you wish,' retorted the Archbishop, 'but unless you graciously consent to make the erasures, most of the Deputies will leave Blois tomorrow. Also, Your Majesty's printers will not print any of the Address.'

Henri, too furious to speak, waved the turbulent prelate from the audience chamber and, almost without realising what he was doing, resumed his life-long habit of going to consult his mother.

Catherine was at her most matter-of-fact. 'The decision, my son, has been made for you. If the printers will not print, there is an end of it unless you wish to rouse the Parisians once more. Would it not be better to get some of the address printed rather than nothing?' Her face became tender, but her tone was self-mocking. 'I should not wish your testimonial to me to be lost to posterity.'

Next day the King summoned the Duke of Guise, his brother the Cardinal and the Archbishop to the castle. He produced a copy of the speech and, without a word, drew his pen through the offending matter. Outside, the sky suddenly darkened, a hailstorm burst and a page-in-waiting hastily brought in a wax taper which he held to light the King. 'And some who were present muttered that the Will of the King and of France was being made and that the taper had been lighted that men should see them breathe their last.'

When the Edict of Union was, as Henri had promised, confirmed, it seemed for the moment that the tide had turned. There were vociferous shouts of 'Long live the King!' which had not been heard anywhere—in Paris or Chartres or Blois—for a considerable time. But there were also cries of 'One religion! One religion!' which warned the King he was expected to keep his word to outlaw Huguenotism. Neither of the Guise brothers trusted him in this matter and the *Clergy* in the private deliberations of their order brought up again the question of the condemnation of Henry of Navarre. The King, however, refused to allow it to be discussed in the full Assembly until Navarre had been summoned to Blois and given a chance of publicly taking the Oath of Union and renouncing Calvinism. The Cardinal of Guise pointed out that

Navarre was a relapsed heretic, as was known to all, and any further summons was unnecessary; but the acrimonious argument was cut short by Navarre's illness. He was suddenly stricken with fever, followed by pleurisy, and for some time it was doubtful if he would recover.

When the news of the illness arrived in La Rochelle, the bells of all the churches rang to call the people to prayer and, though it was night, the entire population made intercession to the Almighty to spare the life of their leader.

As soon as he recovered Navarre wrote to Corisande: 'Twice in twenty-four hours I was so weak that they were obliged to turn me by the help of my sheets and had the illness continued two hours more the worms would have made a great feast of me. Assuredly, my heart, I saw the heavens opened, but I was not deemed good enough to enter them. God still wishes to make use of me.'

At Blois, the atmosphere so far worsened that a Florentine envoy summed it up by: 'The day of the dagger will assuredly come.'

15

The Day of the Dagger

The acrimony engendered by the proceedings of the States-General would, it was generally hoped, be somewhat dispelled by the great social event which was planned to take place in Blois as a prelude to the Christmas festivities—the marriage of the King's niece, Christine of Lorraine, to the young Duke Ferdinand of Tuscany. The hopes were not realised.

On the second day of the festivities, during the State Banquet given to foreign ambassadors, the pages of the guests, several hundred of them, were waiting according to custom in the courtyard of the castle and on the grand staircase which led to the royal apartments. To relieve their *ennui*, they invented a new game. They divided themselves into two parties, Royalists and *Guisards*, and proceeded to see which could invent the wittiest insults.

Words sufficed for a time, but the elegant *mot* soon gave place to the intentionally wounding tirade, and words themselves to blows. In a very short time the fight was so bitter that many were wounded and one, at least, was killed. The uproar spread through the castle and even reached the town. The gates of the castle were shut against the citizens and deputies of the States-General who, led by La Chapelle Marteau, tried to invade it in the belief that Guise was being murdered.

Guise, in fact, was talking to the Queen-Mother. When they heard the tumult, she was the more apprehensive of the two. *'Ce n'est rien,'* he said, and continued their conversation, 'his eyelids lowered that no one might read his thoughts'.

His sister, the Duchess of Montpensier, came up to them and, oblivious of everything but his safety, implored him to escape while he could, for the tumult, she said, had obviously been arranged as a cover for his murder.

'I do not think so,' he replied, 'but even if it were, what could I do, being who and where I am? If I saw Death coming in at the door, I should not try to escape by the window.'

As he spoke he looked at the Queen-Mother who nodded her assent to his insouciance and tried to reassure her goddaughter by saying: 'As long as I am here, Catherine, you need have no fear for your brother. Try to hate my son a little less than you do.'

When the King was told that the fracas had started by the pages of the Cardinal de Bourbon attacking the pages of the Duke of Guise, his only comment was: 'They show more wit than their master.'

After the wedding celebrations were over, the Duchess of Montpensier returned to Paris, taking with her the Duchess of Guise, who was pregnant of her fourteenth child and wished to have her accouchement in the capital. Their last words to Guise before they left Blois were to implore him with tears to consider his safety. He did his best to set their minds at rest. 'There is only one thing to fear,' he told them, 'and I promise you I will guard against it. I will never go alone into the King's cabinet without having my own guard in the anteroom. The twelfth of May taught me that wisdom.'

The resolve, reported to Henri by one of the courtiers present at the parting, gave the King furiously to think. He was sure that Guise would be as good as his word and that his murder would need more careful planning than it had been given. It was even possible that it would have to be committed away from the Château. He spoke to Crillon about it.

Crillon declined with some indignation *'cette office de bourreau'*.

'Sire,' he said, 'I am a soldier, not an assassin. Murder is no work for a man of my quality. But if it is Your Majesty's pleasure that I should challenge the Duke to a duel, I will willingly take my chance of being killed in order to kill him for you.'

'I understand and I respect your scruples,' said Henri, realising that he would have probably to rely on the Forty-Five, after all, to try to repeat the tactics of the twelfth of May.

His next step was to effect a reconciliation with Guise. He swore upon the Host at the altar, according to an historian who witnessed the events of these days, 'a perfect reconciliation and friendship with the Duke and oblivion of all past quarrels. And furthermore he declared that he was resolved to abandon the reins of government to his cousin of Guise and the Queen-Mother, since he desired to concern himself with nothing but praying to God and doing penance.'

Miron, who was in constant attendance on Henri and was still not altogether certain when his near-madness was real and when assumed, noted: 'The King at this time pretended to be greatly absorbed by his devotional exercises, especially as he perceived that M. de Guise was lulled into security thereby. He therefore commanded that a number of small cells should be constructed over his apartment for the accommodation of certain Capuchin friars much in his confidence; and for some days he was so indifferent and absorbed that outwardly he seemed to have lost all animation and feeling.'

But even Miron did not know the real purpose of the cells.

Ten days before Christmas, Catherine was forced to take to her bed. She could no longer resist the weakness brought about by her gout and her obesity, her heavy cold, her troublesome cough and her daily fever—'and with seventy years on top of that' as the Papal Nuncio observed.

Henri regarded it as providential. At last his mother was safely out of the way, as far as interference was concerned, and he could plan practical details. In theory he had reduced the matter to its simplest terms. His only hope of success seemed to lie in repeating the previous tactic and using the *Forty-Five*; and, as Guise would now go nowhere without his own guard, the problem resolved itself into the discovery or invention of some occasion on which he could be legitimately deprived of it. The Duke must also be made to surrender, at least temporarily, the keys of the Castle which were in his custody as Grand Master of the Household.

The solution, once Henri stumbled on it, surprised him by its simplicity. The King's usual room for giving audience, the *cabinet vieux*, was reached through the large Council Chamber, where, on ordinary occasions, when no council was sitting, any nobleman visiting the King was allowed to leave his attendants. If, however, it was occupied for official business, the visitor had to dismiss his entourage at the foot of the outside staircase which led from the courtyard to the Council Chamber. As Guise very seldom attended a meeting of the Council (and had, indeed, been to none at Blois on this occasion) it was at least possible that he would have forgotten the regulation.

The King's next step was to prepare his new councillors for the event. He called a few of them to a private interview and regaled them with a carefully prepared speech rehearsing all the humiliations he had suffered at the hands of the League and of Guise and informing them that Guise intended to force him to abdicate so that he could make himself King. This, Henri suggested, could only be met by the sternest measures. There was no doubt that the Duke deserved to die, but how was the death to be accomplished?

The new Chancellor suggested that Guise should be arrested and put on trial in Paris for high treason.

The King, wondering if he had after all been right in appointing a man who, however admirable his character, had so tenuous a grasp on the realities of politics, explained patiently that no court could be found to convict the Duke and that, in Paris at the moment, it was improbable that he could be arrested and impossible that he could be imprisoned.

Gently the King propelled the discussion in the direction he wished it to go until his advisers, after quoting 'The safety of the State is the supreme Law' and other convenient maxims, reluctantly recommended assassination.

Henri gravely thanked them, promised to ponder their suggestion and dismissed them.

Guise did not lack warnings. On December 21 he received no less than ten anonymous notes informing him that the King was making plans against his life and begging him to leave Blois while there was still time. He reported this at the Hôtel d'Alluye to his brother the Cardinal, the Archbishop of Lyons, La Chapelle Marteau and the Sieur de Mayneville who formed his inner ring of advisers. Were the warnings part of a subtle plan on the King's part to get him to leave the States-General or were they from secret friends alarmed for his safety? He had no doubt that the King wished to kill him; but he was in genuine doubt as to what was the best course for him to take for the good of France.

The Cardinal said: 'I should never presume, my dear brother, to advise you on this. I follow your judgment.'

The Archbishop of Lyons merely quoted the proverb 'Who leaves the table loses the game'.

La Chapelle Marteau said fiercely: 'We are by far the stronger. Let us ensure your safety by imprisoning the little sod as a hostage.'

De Mayneville shouted: 'I agree. The King is also a fool, a tyrant and a madman and we treat him as if we feared and respected him. Let us move against him at once.'

'Call him what you like,' said Guise, 'he wears the crown of St. Louis and that is a power worth more than his armies. Nor will I ever move against it.'

'What then?' asked the Cardinal.

'We have gained what we asked. He has sworn to root out heresy and see that the Faith alone is the religion of France. Let us leave him to do it. I shall resign the Lieutenant-Generalship and go back to Joinville to wait on events.'

'When?'

'Tomorrow.'

That evening Henri asked Guise to accompany him to Vespers. The Duke assumed that the King wished to impress him with his extreme piety and reacted against it by sitting through everything but the *Magnificat* reading a Huguenot pamphlet someone had thrust into his hand on the way to the church. The burden of the work was an analysis of the present troubles of France and an attribution of them to the

King because he did not insist on being obeyed.

The conclusion of it ran: 'His weakness and the ease with which he can be defied are such that any Frenchman today can say as boldly as any foreigner might: "I am not of the King's Party", whereas thirty years ago it would have been a blasphemy, a parricide. Today the King is a "nought", that is to say he has no value in himself but only confers value on the figure to which he is added. He must lose no time in changing such a state of affairs. Nothing should be so preciously preserved by a prince as the fear and respect due to his crown, for once lost they can never be recovered except by such things as create fear, that is by violence and cruelty.'

When they came out of church, Guise passed the pamphlet to the King saying: 'You should read this, sire.'

'What is it, cousin? A new book of devotion?'

'A piece of Huguenot advice. You would find it quite amusing.'

'I do not care to read Huguenot writings.'

'One should know one's enemy.'

Henri made no answer but after the Duke had left him he was seen to dash his hat on the ground and jump on it, quivering from head to foot in an inarticulate frenzy.

On Thursday 22 December, the King and the Duke went to visit the Queen-Mother in her room and stayed for some time chatting with her and eating sweetmeats and discussing plans for the Christmas season. Henri announced that he intended to spend Christmas devoutly visiting the shrine of Notre Dame de Cléry and had arranged to set off, accompanied by Queen Louise, on the morrow about noon.

One of the company in the Queen-Mother's room was

Charlotte de Sauve, Marquise de Noirmoutiers, who, when married to her first husband, M. de Sauve, one of the royal Secretaries of State, had been the most valuable of Catherine's 'flying squadron' of beautiful women who influenced politics through the bedroom. It was Charlotte de Sauve who, in the first days of the marriage of Henry of Navarre and Marguerite de Valois, had been the mistress of the husband and the intimate friend and gossip of the wife, thus completing a curiously constituted triangle which Catherine found an invaluable aid to governing. It was Charlotte who, exercising her supreme skill in arousing jealousy, had set Navarre at odds with Monsieur when their co-operation would have been dangerous to the Throne. Above all, it was Charlotte who had become entangled in all their lives at the crucial moment when King Henri, then Duc d'Anjou, had discovered Margot and Guise in a far-away, unused bedroom in the Louvre and, in a paroxysm of jealous hatred, had forced the Duke's immediate marriage to his present Duchess. Charlotte had understood the tragic personal consequences of that severing of the lovers and through the vicissitudes of the years she had remained their friend, doing what good offices she could. She had in fact come to Blois now not for the reason she had announced—to visit Catherine in her illness—but to try to persuade Guise to leave it. It was what Margot, had she not been so strictly imprisoned at Usson, would have done.

Charlotte, of the broad brow and the sphinx-like smile, could act decisively enough in a political sense if necessity arose:[1] she would indeed have made a more perceptive Secretary of State than her husband. But her placidity, her sensuality and her sense of the ridiculous, accompanied by

[1] As, for example, when she foiled Coligny's attempt to get control of Charles IX. See *The Florentine Woman*, p. 211.

the fact that since she was fourteen she had always been in a position to see how events were manipulated behind the scenes, confirmed her almost exclusive interest to people. She knew the mortal danger Guise was in because she understood why Henri hated him.

Her contribution to the conversation in Catherine's room was of the lightest nature. Her anecdotes and witticisms irritated the King who wanted to involve Guise in a deep political discussion in front of the Queen-Mother and found himself frustrated at every approach to it. Eventually he abandoned the attempt and suggested to the Duke that, as the day was unexpectedly fine and warm for the season of the year, they should continue their discussion strolling round the battlements.

As they left, Charlotte said she was delighted that Guise had accepted her invitation to sup with him. This surprised him, for nothing had been said about such a thing.

The King, once he and the Duke were alone, said: '*Mon cousin*, let us celebrate this Christmas by showing good-will to one another.'

'Sire,' said Guise, 'I have never wished to show you anything but good-will. And now that you have once more sworn to restore the Catholic religion to France you will find nothing but good-will in the Estates.'

'Then let them show it in their deeds! You know that the *Tiers* has asked for a cut of over two million in taxation and since May I have been granted no more than 4,000 francs. How am I to pay my army and, without the army, how am I to put down the Huguenot rebels?'

'There is no doubt that now the Estates are satisfied that

you will devote the money to the enforcement of religion—'

'Instead of giving it to that reprehensible d'Épernon—'

'I neither said nor thought that, sire,' said Guise angrily.

'As I am determined to keep our pact of good-will I will believe you,' said Henri. 'But will you yourself ask the Estates to grant the money needed?'

'How much does your council estimate it at?'

'The war on the Huguenots will cost 700,000 livres a month.'

'You accept this?'

'Certainly. And that is for France alone. Of course, should the Germans invade again or England come to their aid, it would be more. Will you support me in asking for it?'

'I must discuss it with my people, but I think I can promise to.'

He scribbled on a piece of paper: 'For a war in France, 700,000 livres a month are needed,' and put it in his pocket.

'And now, Your Majesty, I have a request to make.'

'Yes? It is one, I trust, which I shall be able to grant.'

'I wish to resign immediately the office of Lieutenant-General which you have been gracious enough to bestow on me and all my other offices except the Governorship of Champagne. And that I pray you to confirm to my son, the Prince of Joinville, after my death.'

Henri was so taken aback that all he could say was: '*Mon cousin*, you are not serious?'

'Perfectly.'

'But it is impossible. Quite impossible.'

'May I ask why?'

'It would throw everything into confusion. Who could take your place?'

'Your Majesty cannot have forgotten that when you were

Duc d'Anjou you were the Lieutenant-General under whom I had the honour to serve. There is nothing you do not know about it and the office itself could remain in abeyance for awhile and be merged with the Crown.'

'No, no, no!'—there was almost a note of alarm in Henri's voice—'I repeat, it is quite impossible. Sleep on it, *mon cousin*, and in the morning I am sure you will agree with me.'

The realisation that there was a real danger that Guise would suddenly leave Court threw Henri into a panic. He had vaguely intended the murder to take place sometime between Christmas and the New Year. Now he must plan it in careful detail for tomorrow. To a certain extent he had fortune on his side. Guise would be involved for the evening—and possibly for the night—with Charlotte. The Queen-Mother was firmly confined to her bed and the hazard of her unexpectedly and inconveniently visiting the King's apartments could be discounted. He had announced that he was leaving for Cléry at noon tomorrow, so that all that was necessary in that respect was to devise a reason for an earlier start. And Guise himself, by his threatened resignation, had given him a perfect excuse to call a meeting of the council at which he had every reason to insist on the Duke's attendance.

His first action was to announce a change of plan for the morrow. Instead of visiting Notre Dame de Cléry, he was going to Noyers, a hermitage on the borders of the forest about six miles from the castle. This would enable him, if he made an early enough start, to perform his devotions there and to return to Blois in time for the council meeting. He ordered his coach for four in the morning and fixed the time for the council for seven to half-past, although he himself would probably not be able to get to it till eight.

As he was leaving so early, he sent his secretary, Revol, to Guise to explain the circumstances and to suggest that, for everyone's convenience, the keys that night should be left with the King. The Duke agreed and without question gave them to the secretary, confirming also that he would attend the meeting of the council, early though it seemed.

Henri next summoned de Laugnac, the Captain of the Forty-Five, under the pretext that he wished all the guardsmen to accompany the royal coach to Noyers; but as soon as de Laugnac was alone with him, he said: 'The time has come to finish what we had to leave undone on the twelfth of May. What will your men say to it?'

'They will, I know, be as happy as I am. Ever since M. de Guise described us to the States-General as rogues and criminals who ought to be disbanded, they have wanted his blood. When are we to have it?'

'Tomorrow morning. Have your men here at five o'clock.'

They discussed the method. At each end of the King's bedchamber were doors leading to his private studies—to the *cabinet vieux* on the one side and to the *cabinet neuf* on the other. Beyond the *cabinet neuf* were the oratory and the Queen's bedroom and to it a passage led direct from the Council Chamber.[2] They decided to station de Laugnac himself with seven picked companions in the *cabinet neuf* to which Guise was to be summoned from the Council Chamber. He would have no retreat except into the King's bedroom and here he could be cut off, in the unlikely event of his surviving

[2] See ground plan in the appendix. Several writers have made events unintelligible by assuming that the King summoned Guise to the *cabinet vieux* instead of to the *cabinet neuf*.

the attack of the eight, by the advance of twelve more who would be with the King in the *cabinet vieux*.

After he had dismissed Laugnac the King sent for Larchant, captain of his *gardes du corps*. With him Henri felt more at ease than with Crillon, the soldier of fortune, or Laugnac, the ruffianly adventurer, for, by dint of many years of faithful service, Larchant had attained the status of a friend. He had been with Henri in Poland and had played a leading part in the adventure of the King's escape. He had watched the long procession of favourites and survived them all. He had coped with the varied rifts within the royal family, understanding Catherine without ever serving her in preference to Henri, treating Monsieur with respectful correctitude as Heir Apparent without ever ceasing to oppose and thwart him in the King's interest, adapting his attitude to the unpredictable vagaries of Margot. He could assume responsibility without appearing to impose his own will and was able to give Henri unpalatable advice in such a way that what from others would have been dismissed as unwarrantable impertinence was from Larchant accepted as humble concern for the King's welfare. But he very seldom did anything but carry out orders promptly and without question and the King knew that, when he spoke to him now, he had no need to give any explanations.

'Tomorrow morning,' said Henri, 'M. de Guise will be attending an early meeting of the council. By half-past six you will have your entire guard drawn up in the courtyard and as he passes through they will ask him to be good enough to plead their cause with me for the payment of the arrears in their wages. By the way, remind me how far they are in arrears.'

'Forty weeks,' said Larchant. 'The men fear they will soon be forced to sell their horses.'

169

'Be sure they tell that to M. de Guise. It will make him see the importance of his intervention.'

'And are there any grounds for hoping,' asked Larchant with a slight smile, 'that you will grant it when he asks it?'

'My dear Larchant,' the King replied, 'I grant it now before he asks it.'

'To take effect immediately?'

'As immediately as I can manage it. You can say it is my gratitude for their services tomorrow.' And he proceeded to discuss with the Captain the further disposition of the guards.

When all the arrangements had been completed, Henri retired to his room with the Sieur de Termes and the secretary, Revol. The choice was not fortuitous. It was a tribute to Épernon who was a relative of Termes and who had, from Angoulême, sent the young and decorative Revol for the King's use. Henri took them both into his confidence and hoped that their approval would have been endorsed by Épernon himself. At midnight he dismissed them with: 'Go to bed now, *mes enfants*. See that du Halde does not fail to call me at four o'clock and be here yourselves at the same hour.'

The warnings to Guise continued. At supper he found another note under his napkin: 'Be on your guard. The King threatens your life.' He scribbled on it: 'He would not dare' and threw it under the table for anyone to find.

Charlotte, when he explained what it was, reproved him. 'You should not be foolhardy, Henry. Why would he not dare?'

'It would mean a rebellion. From north to south the whole country would rise and he would lose his own life.'

'But you would be dead.'

He shrugged. 'That's always a hazard. But, as I say, I do not think he would dare.'

'You have always underestimated his hatred of you.'

'Let us talk of something more pleasant.'

'If it annoys you, I won't speak of it again.'

But when the meal was ended, Charlotte handed him two more notes which she had been keeping for him.

'I asked you not to—'

'Did I say a word?'

'Let us go to bed,' said the Duke and pushed the warnings under the pillow.

At three o'clock he left her and went back to his own rooms, which were on the ground floor of the east wing of the Château. He slept soundly until half-past seven when, realising he would be late for the council meeting, he dressed very hurriedly and, though the weather had grown much colder in the night and sleet was falling, he did not trouble to change the thin grey suit he had worn the day before.

In the royal apartments, the King's first *valet-de-chambre*, du Halde, knocked, as he had been instructed to, on the King's door at four o'clock. One of Queen Louise's women, without opening the door, asked who was disturbing them at such an untimely hour.

'It is du Halde. Tell the King it is four o'clock.'

'Their Majesties are asleep and I cannot disturb them,' said the woman.

'Rouse the King at once or I shall knock so loud that the whole château will be woken.'

Du Halde, like Larchant, was one of Henri's most trusted

servants who had been with him in Poland, and who knew what the King would have wished him to do. Accustomed to all his master's moods and eccentricities as he was, however, even he was not prepared for what followed. The King, who had not been to bed, came to the door immediately in his slippers and dressing-gown and with a candle in his hand and, putting his finger on his lips to enjoin silence, motioned to the valet to follow him. They tiptoed up the little secret staircase to the roof where the cells for the Capuchin monks had been constructed. Into the first of these he pushed du Halde and locked him in. The faithful valet, as he afterwards admitted to Miron, 'had never been more troubled in his life'. Though he had always been prompt to contradict the gossip that the King was mad, he was now forced to reconsider the matter. He became even more mystified and disturbed when, an hour later, he heard Henri bringing seven more people up the stairs one by one and locking each into a separate cell.

The newcomers were the seven of the *Quarante-cinq* who, with de Laugnac, were to commit the actual murder in the *cabinet neuf*. They had, on Henri's instructions to their captain, been told nothing and they were as puzzled as du Halde at their plight. It was not till an hour and a half later, when the first members of the Council were beginning to arrive, that the King, enjoining silence lest the Queen-Mother should be woken, released them and led them down into the *cabinet neuf* where de Laugnac was waiting. The King made an effective little speech, telling them of all the wrongs and humiliations which the Duke of Guise had inflicted on him and concluding: 'I am reduced to such extremity that either he or I must die this very morning. Are you willing to serve me and avenge me by taking his life?'

Their delight was such that they were only by the sternest threats of de Laugnac prevented from compromising the success of the enterprise by exultant shouts; but nothing could prevent one of them, Périac, tapping the King familiarly on the chest and saying in his Gascon patois: *'Cap de Diou, sire, iou lou bous rendis mort!'*

Henri, far from being displeased by the familiarity, stroked Périac's arm and drivelled: 'Take care of yourself. He is very tall and strong and I should be desolated if you were hurt.'

'We can all look after ourselves, Your Majesty,' said de Laugnac.

Leaving the murderers, Henri went to his oratory and commanded two of his chaplains to offer special prayers for 'an enterprise which would make for the repose of the realm'. He offered no enlightenment as to its nature, but the priests, disturbed by the noises which came from the adjoining *cabinet neuf*, peeped through the door and saw de Laugnac and Périac dancing together, Périac with a naked dagger in his hand. They returned to their prayers but offered them, now with personal intensity and conviction, in the opposite sense.

Guise made his way quickly to the wing of the Château which contained the royal apartments. He was late and it was cold and wet and he was attended only by his secretary, two pages and a few gentlemen. At the foot of the Grand Staircase, he found Larchant and the entire *Gardes du Corps* and inquired the reason for such an unusual display. Larchant explained they had come to petition him and he consented to raise the matter that morning. The captain then asked permission for them to wait to learn the decision. Guise consented, assuming that they intended to remain where they were; but no sooner had the door of the Council Chamber closed behind him than Larchant ordered his men to line up in two ranks along the whole length of the staircase and on the landing above, thus barring all access to or egress from the Council Chamber and interposing themselves between it and Guise's suite. At the same moment Crillon ordered all the gates of the Château to be shut.

In the Council Chamber eleven members, including the Cardinal of Guise and the Archbishop of Lyons, had already assembled and were holding various private conversations, though the formal business had not yet begun. They welcomed Guise, whose first request was that the fire should be lighted. The sudden bitter weather had also made the eye beneath his scar water profusely and in his haste he had forgotten a handkerchief. He asked the Clerk of the Treasury to go to the door and ask any of his people who were waiting there to bring him one. The Marshal d'Aumont, one of the Councillors, who at the last moment had been perforce taken into the secret by the King, quickly told one of the royal pages to give the Duke a handkerchief so that he would not have to wait for one of his own.

The Duke thanked the page and requested him also to see whether he could get him some sweetmeats—Damascus raisins or conserve of roses—as in his haste he had forgotten to have his *drageoir*, his silver comfit box shaped like a shell, filled by his own valet. He attributed his faint feeling of nausea to hunger brought on by not having broken his fast. The page returned, somewhat apologetically, with some Brignolles plums which was the only thing he could find.[3] Guise laughed at his embarrassment, ate one, put two in his *drageoir* and threw the rest on the table, inviting the other councillors to help themselves.

The Duke's request for a handkerchief had reached his own suite. Larchant had thought it politic and the message had been passed on to his secretary. The secretary was already sufficiently alarmed by the disposition of the *Gardes du Corps* and wrote a note which he fixed in the corner of the hand-kerchief: 'Monseigneur, save yourself or you are a dead man.' This he gave to one of Guise's pages with instructions to deliver it to the usher of the Council Chamber. When the page returned, saying that he had been refused permission to pass, the secretary, certain that his master was lost, rushed across the courtyard to warn the Duchess of Nemours, Guise's mother. He entreated her to go at once for safety to the Queen-Mother. Hardly had he spoken than twelve of Crillon's Swiss archers under an officer entered the apartment, unceremoniously turned the secretary out of it and placed the Duchess under arrest.

The King, gauging the moment, told Revol to go into the Council Chamber and inform the Duke that he wished to

---

[3] Brignolles plums were the fashionable restorative for the fatigues of love-making.

speak with him in the *cabinet neuf*. The young man obeyed, but he was stopped at the door by one of the Forty-Five who refused to allow him to pass. Although Revol was aware, from the conversation of the previous night, exactly what the arrangements were, the difference between a theoretical discussion and the physical actuality was such as to make him, who had never participated in violence, almost faint. When he returned to tell the King what had happened, Henri said: 'Revol. Mon Dieu, *qu'avez-vous*? How pale you look. You will spoil everything. Rub your cheeks, Revol! Rub your cheeks!' And himself pinching them hard to assist the return of colour, Henri lifted the tapestry *portière* and told the guardian of it to let the secretary pass.

On receiving the summons Guise rose immediately, bowed to his colleagues and, flinging his cloak over his left arm and holding his *drageoir* and handkerchief in his left hand, went through the door leading to the King's bedroom and the *cabinet neuf*. Two of the Forty-Five waiting there saluted him humbly and, as if in respect, followed him.

In five minutes it was over. One of the murderers seized his legs to hamper his movement; another stabbed him in the chest; a third in the throat; Périac buried his dagger in his back; de Laugnac carefully thrust his sword into his groin. With ten wounds and his life fast ebbing, Guise's immense strength and power of will was such that he broke the nose of one of his assailants with his *drageoir* and managed to drag himself, having thrown them all off for the moment, through the door of the King's bedroom. As he advanced with outstretched arms, blinded by the blood pouring from the wound in his forehead, de Laugnac, laughing to the others, unloosened his scabbard and held it low enough for the Duke to trip over. Guise fell to the ground at the foot of the King's bed, faintly breathing the words: *'Mon Dieu! Mon Dieu! ayez pitié de moi!'*; and so died.

The King, when de Laugnac informed him that it was now safe, came into the bedroom and, gazing curiously at the dead body, remarked: 'He looks even taller dead than alive.' He then kicked him in the face.[4]

Having ordered a search to be made of Guise's pockets, Henri was gratified that, in addition to a purse containing twelve gold pieces, there was a scrap of paper bearing the words: 'For a war in France, 700,000 livres a month are required,' which he could show to the Council as proof that the Duke was raising an army to dethrone him.

The Council, as soon as Guise had disappeared through the door, realised, by the commotion and the Duke's cries, what was happening on the other side of it. The Archbishop of Lyons rushed to try to open it and, finding it locked, groaned 'France is lost!' The Cardinal, shouting 'They are killing my brother!', made for the staircase door only to be met by a detachment of the guard who entered and put both prelates under arrest. At the same moment Marshal d'Aumont drew his sword and ordered all his fellow-councillors to take the places they had occupied at the table before the interruption. He counselled patience and submission and extolled the virtues of the King.

In a few minutes the locked door into the royal apartments

[4] This detail is omitted by Miron—doubtless out of loyalty to Henri—in his account *Relation de la Mort de Messieurs les duc et Cardinal de Guise*; but Pierre de l'Estoile notes it in his *Journal*.

was flung violently open and de Laugnac entered, his drawn sword still wet with Guise's blood. The King's voice was heard loudly ordering: 'Open the doors and remove the hangings that all may enter' and de Laugnac gave the command that the entire Council was required by His Majesty in the bedroom.

They found Henri standing near the Duke's body, which was now partially covered by a piece of tapestry. On the dead man's breast was some straw which someone had twisted into the shape of a cross. The King told the councillors: 'At last I am King. The Duke of Guise is dead. Look at him well and know what you may expect if you presume to infringe upon my authority.' With that he dismissed them, ordering Marshal d'Aumont to keep the Cardinal of Guise and the Archbishop of Lyons in strict confinement.

The Cardinal de Bourbon meanwhile had been arrested in his bed. The old man was now brought, weeping and apprehensive, into the Royal presence. The mere sight of the titular King of the League threw Henri into an even greater fury. He called the terrified prelate all the insulting names that came to his tongue, including *'L'âne rouge'*. 'You pathetic puppet, you pretentious imbecile,' the King concluded, 'but for your age, I would do the same to you. Even now, I have not quite made up my mind what to do with you. *Mort de Dieu* to think of your aspiring to become the second person in the kingdom! I will make you so small that the least in my realm shall be greater than you!' Then, giving orders that the Cardinal was eventually to be held under arrest in his room, the King left him alone for half-an-hour to contemplate the body of Guise.

*   *   *

At ten o'clock Henri, dressed in his most elaborate and festal attire, set out for the Church of St. Sauveur to offer his thanks at Mass. On the way, he called on his mother in her bedroom. Catherine's chest was giving her great pain and she was finding breathing difficult. The Bishop of Paris was reading his breviary to her. Henri asked her how she was feeling. She had to admit that she felt worse than she had the day before.

Henri replied: 'You will be pleased to know that I have never felt so well. I am King of France at last. I have just had the King of Paris killed.'

She seemed not to understand him, so he repeated it.

At last Catherine said, with a look of utter despondency: 'God grant, my son, that you have not made yourself King of Nothing!'[5]

---

[5] It is interesting that Christopher Marlowe in his *Massacre at Paris*, first produced in the January of 1593—four years after Guise's murder—is almost the only English author to make Catherine disapprove of the action, as she did. He makes her say:

> I cannot speak for grief . . .
> My son, thou art a changeling, not my son;
> I curse thee and exclaim thee miscreant
> Traitor to God and to the realm of France . . .
> The Protestants will glory and insult;
> Wicked Navarre will get the crown of France;
> The Popedom cannot stand: all goes to wreck.

16

Aftermath

Next day, Christmas Eve, the news of the murder reached Paris. One of Guise's servants managed to leave Blois before the enforcement of the order that no one was allowed through the gates without a permit signed personally by the King. The man, reporting to Guise's cousin, the Duke of Aumale, at the Hôtel de Guise, was not at first believed. 'Our cowardly weakling of a king would never dare,' Aumale said. Nevertheless, after consulting the Duchess of Montpensier, he notified the *Seize*, who held a hurried meeting in the Hôtel de Ville and immediately sent off an envoy to Orléans to obtain verification. Long before the messenger returned, however, several confirmations of the event arrived and by nightfall the tragic truth was generally accepted.

There was unprecedented panic and confusion in the city. Guards were posted at all the gates and watch-fires were lighted in the main squares. Every church was packed to overflowing at Midnight Mass where, from the pulpits, the news was officially proclaimed and the preachers vied with one another in their denunciations of the King, anticipating the judgment of the Sorbonne that obedience was no longer due to him and that to kill him would be a meritorious act. In some of the churches, the eulogies on 'the martyred Duke' provoked the congregations to shouts of *'Nous n'avons pas de roi! Maudit soit le tyran!'*

When Mass was over, the crowds poured through the streets, accompanied by the principal officers of the municipality, to the Hôtel de Montmorency where Guise's wife and sister were in residence. In spite of the hour the people clamoured for the Duchess of Guise's appearance on the balcony so that they might assure her of their sympathy and their determination to avenge her loss. Her condition was pitiable and, in the eighth month of her pregnancy, not without danger. She had fainted at the first rumour of the murder and now, though she insisted on appearing for a few seconds supported by her women, she swooned again and had to be carried back insensible to her bedroom.

The Duchess of Montpensier had been even more gravely affected by the news. Her doctor feared a stroke. Her face became for a few minutes suffused with passion and then she lay for a long time motionless and livid. After a short interval her cries of despair, horror and rage rang through the Hôtel as she tore her hair and uttered blood-curdling imprecations on Henri. She, too, now needed the support of her attendants, as she appeared before the people. She exhorted them to rise and destroy 'the treacherous little sodomite' and, raising her hands above her head, swore that henceforth her own life should be dedicated to nothing but revenge.

In Blois Henri was completing the work he had begun and held discussions with his intimates about the fate of the Cardinal of Guise and the Archbishop of Lyons. They had been imprisoned in a small room lacking bed, table or chairs and were guarded by four of the *Quarante-cinq*. They had been allowed no food, according to Henri's careful instructions, but raw fish, as it was a fasting season.

The Cardinal, overwhelmed by the murder of the brother he had so loved and admired, seemed to have lost all initiative, but the Archbishop complained angrily to Larchant with the result that about eleven o'clock at night two coarse mattresses were brought in for them to sleep on and the guard was withdrawn from their room so that they might have some privacy. Immediately they made their confessions to each other and gave and received absolution before they fell into a sleep of exhaustion.

At midnight word was brought to the King that, in the morning, the whole Order of the Clergy intended to petition him in person for their president, the Cardinal's release. In a rage, Henri said: 'Then let him die before they arrive.' The difficulty was to find anyone who was willing to kill him. None of the Forty-Five, not even de Laugnac, would risk the sacrilege of killing a priest. Larchant recoiled in horror when Henri suggested it to him. Eventually de Termes, Épernon's relative, discovered a volunteer—Michael du Guast, a distant connection of the King's first favourite of long ago, who had been reprimanded by the Cardinal for cheating at cards.

At eight o'clock in the morning of Christmas Eve, du Guast entered the room in which the prelates were imprisoned and, making a low reverence, said to the Cardinal: 'Monseigneur, the King desires your presence.'

'Both of us?'

'No, Monseigneur, I am only charged to summon you.'

The Archbishop pressed the Cardinal's hand and whispered: 'Commend your soul to God.'

The Cardinal said: 'Father, give me your blessing,' and fell on his knees before him. The Archbishop, so moved that it was only with great difficulty that he could pronounce the formula, blessed him and the Cardinal rose and was led away.

As soon as the door closed, du Guast said: *'Cardinal, il faut mourir'* and led him to a small gallery where six of the Forty-Five were waiting.

The Cardinal asked for a few moments to prepare himself for death and kneeling with his face turned towards a recess in the wall he commended his soul to God. Before he had finished his prayers, du Guast stabbed him in the back, and the Forty-Five, who whatever their scruples in killing him had none in mangling the corpse, so mutilated the body that it became almost unrecognisable. Eventually it was wrapped in some rough sacking and carried into a room near the castle chapel where the body of his brother, covered with green serge cloth, lay on the floor.

Later in the day, by order of the King, both bodies were burnt and the ashes scattered on the river Loire so that nothing remained which could be treated as a relic and there was no grave to become a place of pilgrimage.

When news of the second murder reached Paris, the citizens' fury passed even the bounds of the previous day. Portraits of the Duke and the Cardinal, 'martyrs for Jesus and the public weal', were put on the altars of the churches, packed continuously with congregations responding with sobs and imprecations to the bitter denunciations of the preachers. Everywhere the royal arms were pulled down and images of the King broken and thrown in the mud. In the church of the Augustinians the two great paintings of the King founding the Order of the *Saint-Esprit* were slashed to shreds and in the church of Saint Paul the marble tombs which Henri had erected in memory of his *mignons*, Quélus, Maugiron and Saint-Mégrim,[1] were smashed to pieces and the embalmed corpses thrown in the Seine. Processions of men, women and children, barefoot for penance in the bitter weather, chanted the *Miserere* and carried torches which, on the pavement outside Notre Dame, they dashed to the ground with the cry: 'So may God extinguish the House of Valois!' Throughout the twelve days of Christmas the demonstrations continued. On December 28, the Feast of the Holy Innocents, a preacher told his congregation that he had discovered that 'Henri de Valois' was an anagram for 'Vilain Hérode' and on New Year's Day the parish priest of another called upon his congregation to take an oath to endeavour 'to the last sou of their money and to the last drop of their blood' to avenge the murdered brothers.

On the eve of the Epiphany, the widowed Duchess of Guise gave birth to a posthumous son, who was adopted by the city and carried in state to Notre Dame where the sheriffs stood sponsors at his baptism and where he was given the name of Paris Alexandre de Lorraine. A deputation was then appointed to go to Blois to demand the liberation of La Chapelle Marteau and other members of the League and the envoys first publicly made their wills before trusting themselves to the clutches of the 'execrable traitor and perjurer'.

Henri made light of the situation. He said: 'I know those demagogues of Paris better than any man in the realm and after a little bravado and lament for their *Roi Guisard*, they will fall at my feet and I shall know how to make them rue their mistakes.'

[1] *The Last of the Valois*, p. 188.

He sent a detachment of troops to arrest the Duke of Mayenne who was in Lyons. Mayenne, increasingly lethargic with his growing corpulence and very aware of his inferiority to the Duke as a soldier, was reluctant to assume the leadership which had now fallen on him, but his determination to avenge his brothers overcame any hesitation. Brandishing a naked sword, he rode bareheaded into the principal square of Lyons and publicly swore to take vengeance by himself spilling the blood of the royal murderer. Then, warned of the approach of the King's troops, he rode to the safety of Orléans to await his summons by the Parlement of Paris to be invested as chief of the League with the title of Lieutenant-General of the State and Crown of France. Henri replied by proclaiming him a traitor and depriving him of all his honours.

When news of the two murders reached Rome, on 5 January 1589, the Pope, according to his temperament, sharply discriminated between them. Of the death of Guise he said: 'The Duke was in his power and the King was master and could do what he wished against his subjects without having to render an account to anyone but God; but after the King was reconciled to the Duke to have him butchered is not an act we can praise, for it was not justice but murder and it grieves us that he should have committed such a sin. What the King should have done was to have arrested him and put him on trial and then have done what he wished because he is king. Thus all would have been well done.'

But of the death of the younger brother, Sixtus said: 'Our sorrow is so unspeakable that we cannot find words to describe it, for the sacrilegious crime which has caused it is quite unheard of. By the order of the King of France, a Cardinal has been killed, a Cardinal Priest has been killed and one who was at the same time Archbishop of Rheims. He has been butchered without trial by civil authority, like any ordinary man without consideration of his episcopal rank and without sanction of the Holy See.'

The Pope was not mollified by Henri's attempt to bribe him by offering to his nephew the vacant Cardinalate or by the King's flippant postscript: 'I forgot to inform Your Holiness that it was necessary to act as I have done because Cardinal Guise had the impudence to say that he did not intend to die until he had held my head while his sister cut my hair to make a monk of me.'

After some consideration the Pope laid it upon Henri, under pain of major excommunication, to set at liberty within ten days the Cardinal de Bourbon and the Archbishop of Lyons and, within sixty days, himself to appear in Rome either by proxy or in person.

17

The Death of Catherine

Catherine, though she failed to persuade Henri to release the Cardinal de Bourbon, managed to get permission to visit him and on New Year's Day she was carried in her chair to the apartment where he was held under house-arrest. He was so overcome with emotion at seeing her that he threw himself on his knees at her feet, kissing and clasping her hands and weeping copiously. She answered his tears with her own and tried to speak comfortable words to him.

But gradually his mood changed. Self-pity for his own precarious position dwarfed all other emotions. He went so far as to accuse her of being instrumental in inducing the Guises to trust the King and thus to have come to Blois at all. 'Madame! Madame! This is your device!'

Catherine was at first too taken aback to answer, but as he continued: 'This is your doing! You have slain us all!' she replied angrily: 'Listen to me, Monseigneur. It had nothing whatever to do with me. I knew nothing at all of what my son intended and I should have done everything in my power to prevent it if I had.'

But he was past listening and continued shouting at her:

'It is your doing! You have lured us all to death!'

'May God visit me with His eternal damnation if I devised or approved of what my son has done,' said Catherine. At last, as his accusations grew wilder and his tone more intemperate, she said to her attendants: 'O God, this is too much! I have no strength left. Take me away.'

They carried her back to her room and put her to bed, from which she never again rose.

Next day she made her will, disinheriting Margot and leaving her hereditary estates to her grandson, Charles de Valois, the illegitimate son of Charles IX and Marie Touchet.[1] She then asked for a priest, as her own chaplain had, with many others precipitately left Blois because of their mistrust of the King's intentions. They found her the Abbé of Charlieu, Julien de Saint-Germain, a devout man and a distinguished theologian, who heard her confession, gave her absolution and was able to comfort her greatly until she asked his name. When he told her she said emphatically but without fear: 'Then I am certainly dying.'

A year ago her astrologer, Ruggieri, had warned her 'to beware of Saint-Germain' as it would betoken her death. As a result she had not only been careful never to visit Saint-Germain but had even left her apartments in the Louvre and taken up residence in the Hôtel de Soissons because the palace was in the parish of St. Germain l'Auxerrois.

During the whole of Wednesday 4 January Catherine lay insensible but in the night her sufferings again became intense nor, though conscious, did she regain the power of speech. She died about midday on the Thursday, the Eve of the

[1] See The Last of the Valois, p. 70.

Epiphany, in Henri's arms. An autopsy performed that evening established that her death was due to what her physician described as peri-pneumonia which brought on apoplexy. But it also revealed 'a condition of health in her bodily organs which, if the grace of God had kept her from pleurisy, would have given her many years of life'.

Catherine was killed, literally and symbolically, by the Cardinal de Bourbon. Her visit to him had been undertaken in defiance of her doctor's orders and her exposure to the cold, damp passages of the castle on that freezing mid-winter day had precipitated the crisis of her illness, quite apart from the unendurable strain of the conversation. And, in a deeper sense, the fatal interview had destroyed her will to live, for it epitomised her failure. Her idolised son, for whom she had spent her whole life, had, at this last, destroyed all that she had built, rejected everything she had taught him.

At the moment when the unification of France as a Catholic country was for the first time in his life a practical possibility, he had chosen to prevent it in the interests of his private and personal feud with the only great man the turbulent times had produced. In her support of Guise, she had given the Valois monarchy its last chance of survival. By the assassination of Guise, her son had not only revealed himself as everything the Parisians had accused him of being as a man but he had made himself as she had heart-brokenly predicted 'King of Nothing'. She, even had she had the strength, could do nothing to avert the doom of France, faced with an interminable civil war. It was best to die.

When she was dead, Henri took into his own keeping the celebrated talisman she wore round her neck which was reputed to confer the power of divination. It was said to be made of several metals fused together under astrological combinations based on the date of her birth, mixed with human blood and the blood of a hart. It was covered with the drawings of several demons and with magical formulae. A few days later the King had it broken to pieces.

As Paris was in the hands of the League which, despite the Queen-Mother's recent popularity, shared the Cardinal de Bourbon's mistake about her implication in Guise's death, Catherine could not be buried beside her husband at Saint-Denis in the exquisite tomb which she had built for them in the chapelle de Valois. She was temporarily interred in a niche near the High Altar of the Church of Saint Sauveur in Blois.

Dr. Cavriana, her Florentine physician, wrote what might be considered her justest epitaph: 'She died with great repentance of her sins against God. We all remain without light or counsel or consolation and, to tell the truth, with her died what kept us alive. From now on we must turn our thoughts elsewhere and find some other support. The kingdom will suffer more than is believed now that the King remains without his greatest and most necessary support. God help him!'

But one of the preachers of the League in Paris proclaimed: 'The Queen-Mother is dead. In her life she did much good and much evil. The question is whether the Catholic Church should pray for her, since she so often supported heresy, although at the end she is said to have upheld our Holy League and not to have consented to the death of our good princes. So I shall say this. If you wish to say a *Pater* or an *Ave* for her you may do so. If not, it does not much matter. I leave it to your own judgment.'

18

Brothers-in-Arms

Once Guise was dead, the King's first thought was to ally himself to the Huguenots and to acknowledge Henry of Navarre as heir to the throne. His immediate project to make a formal treaty with the Calvinist cantons of Switzerland and to call in 20,000 German Protestant *reiters* to take Paris was only prevented by the violent protests of the Marshal de Retz, who told him bluntly that such an action would cause every Catholic soldier in his army to desert and, as half the principal towns of the kingdom had already rejected the royal authority, he would soon cease to be King of France in anything but name. Henri, recognising the strength of native Catholicism,[1] swore publicly for the third time to enact the Edict of Union and exterminate heresy in his dominions. This, however, was nothing but a blind to deceive Catholics. Privately he sent a special envoy to Elizabeth of England to ask for the help of the English fleet on the coasts of France and of her army in the Low Countries to divert the attention of Philip of Spain

[1] 'In fact, the sympathies of the whole country were Leaguer and the isolated exceptions prove little beyond the fact that certain individual governors were loyal and strong.'—Maurice Wilkinson: *A History of the League*.

who was, of course, a member of the League. The English Ambassador, on Elizabeth's behalf, 'promised on the word of a queen, in case he came to a downfall that she would help him rise again' and announced that he could shortly expect 4,000 English troops under her rising favourite, the Earl of Essex. In the meantime, she suggested, the King should approach Navarre.

Henri's first steps in this direction were immediately known to the Papal Legate, who wrote to the Vatican: 'The King is preparing to treat Catholics as his deadly enemies and plans to recruit troops from Germany, England and other Protestant states to maintain Huguenotism, so that we shall soon see France inundated with Lutherans and Calvinists.' Henri's own reply to the Legate's protests was short and to the point: 'I would make an alliance with the Turks if it was necessary to keep my throne.'

To facilitate a *rapprochement* with his brother-in-law, Henri recalled Épernon, who arranged a secret treaty with Navarre, by which, in return for the acknowledgment of him as Heir Presumptive and the cession of Saumur to the Huguenots, he promised to support Henri and to provide him at once with 1,200 picked cavalry and 2,000 infantry.

The day after this arrangement had been made, at the beginning of April, Henri transferred the Court to Tours, since he considered Blois no longer safe for him, and, at the same time, he issued an order that the Parlement of Paris should hold its sittings in Tours from April 22.

Mayenne's answer was to organise a new Government in the capital. A Council of Forty became an interim legislative assembly; the Duke of Aumale was nominated President and a new seal was cut, with the *fleur-de-lys* on one side and an empty throne on the other. The first act of the new government was to reduce the existing taxation by a third; the second was to authorise Mayenne to attack Blois, Amboise and Tours —the only towns loyal to the King—in order to liberate the Cardinal de Bourbon, the Archbishop of Lyons, Le Chapelle Marteau and other imprisoned deputies from the now-dissolved States-General.

The Papal Legate made one last attempt at reconciliation. 'Think, sire,' he urged Henri, 'before you incur the anathema of Holy Mother Church by your blasphemous league with princes accursed, alien and heretic. Remember your solemn oath, three times sworn, to maintain the Edict of Union and annihilate heresy.'

Henri, seeing the necessity to play for time, admitted that his conscience was troubled and promised to set the prisoners free, to confirm the princes of the League in their respective governments and to grant a general amnesty.

But at the same time he sent a message to the Duchess of Montpensier ordering her to leave Paris immediately or when he arrived at the head of his troops 'he would have her publicly burnt alive'.

The Duchess sent a reply by his messenger that she was under the impression that burning alive was the conventional penalty for sodomy and that it therefore applied to him rather than to her. Nevertheless, she said, she would do everything in her power to prevent 'that perfidious monster, once, by Divine wrath, King of France' from ever entering the capital.

On April 30, in the garden at Plessis-les-Tours where, twenty years earlier, Henri had committed his cause to the then-beloved Margot,[2] he now welcomed her husband as his

[2] *The Florentine Woman*, p. 165.

saviour. If the old occasion was the beginning of tragedy, the present encounter was the culmination of high comedy. 'The crush was so great,' wrote a spectator, 'that their majesties remained for the space of a quarter of an hour within four yards of each other without being able to embrace. Their salutations and greetings were at length achieved with a marvellous demonstration of gladness. The people were so transported at the sight that they continued their acclamations *Vive le roi et le roi de Navarre!* without intermission for the space of half-an-hour.'

Navarre chose his words with care. He knelt to Henri and, with eyes brimming with the tears that came to him so easily, said: 'From today I shall die content whatever death may befall me, since God has given me grace to look upon my king's face again.'

Henri, whose tears were usually dependent on self-pity, prepared for them by an emotional recital. '*Mon frère*,' he said, 'I have done unheard-of things to promote the embellishment, tranquillity and glory of Paris. I have filled the universities with learned men. I have respected the Sorbonne, honoured the Parlement, adorned the public buildings and augmented the commerce of the city. I have lived in Paris rather as a citizen than as King. In return her clergy have calumniated me, her preachers have wrested my good name from me, the Sorbonne has pretended to release all my subjects from their vows of allegiance. The people of Paris have revolted, stolen my treasures, suborned my officers, killed my Swiss, attacked my bodyguard, broken my seals, burned the escutcheons of my arms, defaced my effigies and seized my artillery to turn against me. Behold therefore, *mon frère*, those who, under detestable pretexts, have rebelled against their anointed prince and rendered themselves odious to man and God! It is to drive out of France—as they have driven me from Paris—these accursed traitors that I have summoned you! It is to defend this noble crown, of which you are the lawful heir, that I now command you to join your forces to mine so that, with the sword God has placed in my hand, we may deliver the people and vindicate our sacred rights!'

The tears of the King now vied with those of Navarre, as the Béarnais drew his sword and swore never to rest until Henri was 'supreme once more in the halls of the Louvre'.

That night, Navarre wrote to Corisande: 'No power on earth can now prevent me from attaining my destiny, since God guides and walks with me. It is His will still to make me His instrument.' But to his royal brother-in-law he gave more mundane advice. To Henri's complaint that he was excommunicated, Navarre replied: 'Then we must conquer as soon as we can, for in that case you will get your absolution absolutely. Let us march direct on Paris, without troubling ourselves about the towns Mayenne has taken.' Then, in an attempt to cheer the lugubrious King: 'Remember, even one Henri is worth more than a beggarly Carolus.'[3]

Both Henries, however, decided to take no action until they had procured overwhelming superiority. 20,000 German *reiters* and 12,000 Swiss were hired, which, added to the 3,000 Huguenots and 3,000 mercenaries provided by Épernon, swelled the tiny royal forces to an army of 40,000 men, equipped with ample artillery, ready to take and eager to sack Paris.

Mayenne, returning rapidly from his victorious campaign in the country to defend the capital had little more than 3,000 trained soldiers, though the citizens of Paris organised them-

[3] In the current coinage a *Henri* was a gold piece, a *Carolus* a copper coin of little value. Mayenne's name, it will be remembered, was Charles.

selves into fighting companies which brought the defenders to a total of nearly 10,000. Strong entrenchments were constructed in the faubourgs St. Germain, St. Jacques, St. Marcel, St. Honoré and St. Denis. But the odds were impossible. The Spanish Ambassador thought that the city might hold out for a week, but the *Politiques* leaders with the King gave it no more than three days at most, and Coligny's son, at the head of a Huguenot detachment, announced with satisfaction that, within five days, so many Catholics would be hanged in Paris that wood for the gibbets would have to be fetched from the forest of Vincennes.

On the evening of the last day of July, 1589, the two kings looked down on the doomed city from the hill of St. Cloud.

'It is almost a crime,' said Henri de Valois, 'to destroy so fine a city. Nevertheless there is nothing else for it. Only so can the rebels be taught obedience.'

Henry of Navarre, reflecting on the ironic turn of events by which what was regarded as the ultimate enormity of the Huguenots—Coligny's calling in of the German *reiters* to sack Paris[4]—was now the official policy of the French crown, could not resist saying: 'I can assure you, brother, that the *reiters* will give the Parisians a lesson they will never forget.'

They fixed the following Wednesday, 2 August, for the assault.

[4] *See The Florentine Woman*, p. 114.

19

Brother Clement

Jacques Clement was a young Dominican friar attached to the great house of the Order of Preachers in the Rue St. Jacques.[1] Twenty-two years ago he had been born in a village near Sens, about seventy miles from Paris and, at eighteen, he had been a soldier in the army of the League. He had never managed to obliterate from his memory the day when, as a boy of nine, he had been forced to watch the atrocities of the German *reiters* as they burnt, looted and raped their way across the countryside of his native Champagne in support of the Huguenots; and his later offer of his sword to Guise had been a simple acknowledgment of an indelible hatred.

The inconclusive chaos of the continuing war, however, disturbed him and eventually it conflicted with that other side of his nature which, also since his childhood, had attracted him to the religious life. At the end of the 1585 campaign, he entered the Dominican priory at Sens as a novice.

He was still at Sens when in the autumn of 1587 the Germans were again invading France. They had gathered at

[1] Because of this geographical position, the Dominicans in Paris were sometimes referred to as Jacobins.

Montargis, a mere thirty miles from Sens, when Guise fell on them and could have destroyed them had they not, by the King's orders, been protected by Épernon and conducted to the frontier in safety. It was at that moment that Clement's suspicion of the King's religion took root. To him, it was obvious that true devotion to Catholicism was synonymous with the League and that Henri's curious practices, with their overtones of masochistic sensuality and *récherché* delight in vestments, were scarcely less heretical than the bleak pride of Calvinism. Clement at least was not surprised at the discovery that the holder for the missal in the King's private chapel at Vincennes was a naked Dionysus in solid gold or that the paten was engraved with a love scene between Achilles and Patroclus.

Having once perceived the weakness of the King's Catholicism, Clement was less surprised than most people[2] when Henri broke his thrice-sworn oath and betrayed not only his faith by his alliance with French Huguenotism but his country by calling in the same German marauders whose previous invasions he had, under his mother's influence, spent most of his reign in repelling.

By this time Clement was in Paris where the matter was one of extreme practical urgency. The young friar, though comparatively late in entering the Order, showed himself so outstanding a theologian as well as so disciplined in his asceticism that the Prior of Sens was of the opinion that a great light had arisen and that, for the honour of the Dominicans, it was his duty to send the paragon to complete his studies in the capital.

[2] The Pope, for instance, who to add to his own poor judgment of men and events seems to have been badly advised by his nuncios, had a fit when he received the news. The French envoys had to retire from Rome to Venice, since their mere proximity threatened a return of the convulsion that nearly cost His Holiness his life.

The impact of life in a city awaiting destruction by the Germans was crucial, not indeed in changing Clement but in reinforcing his convictions.

In one respect he was, indeed, unique in the priory. He actually believed the Christian faith. His desire for Heaven outweighed any earthly ambitions and he was prepared to abide by Christ's paradox: 'Whosoever shall save his life shall lose it but whosoever shall lose his life for My sake shall save it.' It was the charter of martyrdom and again took him back to his childhood where one of his earliest memories was the great picture in the cathedral of Sens, dedicated to St. Stephen, representing the first Christian martyr gazing at a vision of Heaven while he was being done to death.

Another consequence of Clement's simple belief was that he had no respect for secular greatness. He accepted absolutely St. Paul's teaching: 'Ye see your calling, brethren, how that not many wise men after the flesh, not many mighty, not many noble are called; but God hath chosen the foolish things of the world to confound the wise and God hath chosen the weak things of the world to confound the things which are mighty and the base things of the world and the things which are despised hath God chosen, yea and the things which are not, to bring to naught things that are.' And the friar found this revolutionary view emphasised each day in chapel as he chanted the *Magnificat*, the Mother of God's definition of God: 'He hath showed strength with His arm and scattered the proud in the imagination of their hearts; He hath put down the mighty from their seat and exalted them of low degree; He hath filled the hungry with good things and the rich He hath sent empty away.'

*　　　*　　　*

In Paris, the terms of the King's excommunication having been officially proclaimed from the doors of Notre Dame, copies were posted in the streets, with the reminder that the killing of this *ci-devant* King, 'outcast of the monarchs of Europe', was not only 'lawful and expedient' but, in the circumstances, 'acceptable to God'. In addition to 'Vilain Hérode', the appellation 'Henri Dévalé' was invented by the preachers who urged that 'the death of that execrable tyrant would mean the death of heresy'. The relics of the saints, including the Crown of Thorns from the Sainte Chapelle (which St. Louis had built to house it) and the piece of the True Cross from the Cathedral, were carried in solemn procession through the streets, followed by crowds in mourning, led by Guise's widow and his sister. Madame de Montpensier, indeed, clad only in a penitential sheet, insisted, in spite of the now-crippling weakness in her ankles, on making a solitary pilgrimage to the Cemetery of the Innocents, calling on the citizens to find some one who would deputise for her as Judith and secure the head of Holofernes.

The problem which beset the young Dominican posed itself in theological terms. It was not whether it was lawful to kill an excommunicated heretic. It was whether it was permissible for a friar in Holy Orders to do so. Under the seal of confession, he consulted his superior, Prior Bourgoing, as to whether it would be a mortal sin for him to destroy the King. The Prior answered that, having regard to all the circumstances, mortal sin was not involved but that the striking of the blow by a Religious would be an 'irregularity' which would lead to the suspension of his ecclesiastical functions. This Clement found no deterrent. Once Henri was dead, he assumed that he himself would immediately be killed and thus gain the coveted crown of martyrdom. He asked the Prior to arrange a meeting with Madame de Montpensier.

She received him with her accustomed enthusiasm slightly tempered with awe: he seemed to be an answer to prayer. But her promise to procure a Cardinal's Hat for him as a token of her gratitude showed him how far she was from understanding his motives. His wish to discuss matters with her and her brother was because both she and Mayenne could enlighten him on details of the Court and its etiquette so that, in that world unfamiliar to him, he would not make some foolish mistake which, at the last moment, might bar him from the King's presence.

In making his preparations, his experience as a soldier aided his endeavour as a Religious to fulfil Christ's command to His followers to be 'as wise as serpents' and His warning, in His parable of the king preparing for war, against beginning an enterprise without making most careful plans for it and meticulously counting the cost. This parable had always appealed to the soldier in Clement, who had in fact carried with him into the priory a sense of military discipline which was responsible for his nickname 'le Capitaine Jacques'. His first words to Mayenne were to insist that, humanly speaking, the safety of Paris and the survival of Catholicism in France, were doomed beyond any hope.

Mayenne offered to have three hundred of the leading Royalist sympathisers in Paris arrested and held as hostages for Clement's safety, but the friar was adamant in his opposition to such a step. In the first place, he said, he had no wish for safety. He was offering his own life to God as reparation for any sin he might unwittingly commit by literally obeying the Church's teaching about excommunicated heretics. In the second place, he urged, such an action as the mass-arrest of three hundred notables would inevitably arouse suspicion and therefore might increase his difficulties in reaching the King at all.

The pious hopes that Mayenne and his sister expressed that God would protect His servant by rescuing him in some supernatural fashion served only to convince Clement either that their theology was minimal or that they considered him a visionary half-wit. Nor did he find them of any practical use. He courteously rejected Mayenne's offer to provide a forged letter to gain him immediate access to the King, because this seemed to him a conventional passport to disaster. He preferred to rely on his own contacts.

One of his friends was the son of the Sieur de Portail who had succeeded Ambroise Paré as the King's first surgeon. Young Portail had been imprisoned by the *Seize* in the Bastille, more on account of his name than because of anything he had done in the Royal interest, and Clement had visited him regularly in his confinement. He now asked him for an introduction to another Royalist prisoner, Achille de Harlay, First President of the *Parlement* of Paris.

De Harlay, though a Catholic, was opposed to the League and on the morrow of the Day of the Barricades had told Guise that 'it was a great pity when the servant chased away the master'. After Guise's death he had attended the service at St. Bartholomew's when the preacher asked the congregation to pledge themselves to vengeance 'to the last *sou* of their money and the last drop of their blood'.

The preacher had noticed him and cried: 'Raise your hand, M. le Président; raise it much higher; raise it higher still, if you please, so that all the people may see it.' And Achille de Harlay had raised it, well knowing that, had he not, he would not have left the church alive. He was sent to the Bastille, for his own safety as much as anyone else's, a few days later.

When Portail approached him with Clement's request, the President expressed himself as perfectly ready to see the friar and asked what kind of man he was. Portail told him truly enough that, as far as his personal knowledge went, Clement was much respected at his Priory, that he was devoted to his religion—his visits to the Bastille were in fulfilment of Christ's command to comfort the sick and the imprisoned— and that he did not meddle in politics.

The friar's appearance and conversation confirmed the favourable impression which Portail's description of him had given to the President. He was hesitant and humble and quite clearly concerned about the fate of Paris as a city, which he made the excuse for his visit. He knew, so he told the President, that a group of Parisians, consisting of Royalist Catholics, Leaguers, some secret Huguenots and several influential *Politiques*, in order to avoid the destruction of the finest capital of the west by bombardment, were prepared to open one of the gates, provided the King, in return, would issue an order prohibiting the employment of his artillery.

The President would understand that, in so secret and urgent a matter, it was necessary for someone to see His Majesty in person. Clement himself had undertaken the mission, but success was obviously impossible unless he could obtain a safe-conduct which would allow him to pass the outposts of the royal army. Would the President consider giving him one?

De Harlay, after the conventional request for more details which he was too much a man of the world to expect the friar to give, provided the pass, carefully written in his own hand.

*　　　*　　　*

After a day and a night spent in the Priory, Clement heard Mass and communicated on Sunday, 31 July, and at about two o'clock in the afternoon set off on the road to St. Cloud. On the way, he was overtaken by M. la Guesle, the Attorney-General, who, seeing a young friar walking between two soldiers, asked them whether he was their prisoner. Clement explained that he had merely fallen in with them by accident and that, as he himself had once been a soldier, he had asked to be allowed to accompany them as far as St. Cloud. He retained his interest in military matters.

Why was he going to St. Cloud?

He had a very important message to deliver to His Majesty.

The Attorney-General laughed at the friar's ingenuousness. There was no possibility whatever, he said, of an interview with the King. He had better entrust to la Guesle whatever message he had and the lawyer, if he considered it sufficiently important, would pass it on to the King.

'I have no authority,' said the friar, 'to divulge secrets to anyone but those for whom they are intended.'

'Obviously,' said la Guesle, 'it must be an important secret to be entrusted to a young prig of a Jacobin.'

Calmly Clement drew from his sleeve de Harlay's missive and said: 'The First President was good enough to provide me with a safe conduct.'

La Guesle, who was quite familiar with de Harlay's writing, examined it carefully and immediately changed his attitude to the friar. He insisted on him mounting his horse behind him and riding pillion to St. Cloud. In the course of their conversation, Clement told him that young Portail had introduced him to de Harlay and, immediately on arrival at St. Cloud, la Guesle went to the elder Portail to ask him to interview the Dominican. The King's surgeon did so, putting many intimate questions about his son, all of which Clement answered so satisfactorily as further to convince everyone of his genuineness. La Guesle thereupon took him under his patronage, insisted that he lodge with him and informed the King of his arrival. On being told that the Dominican was young and handsome, Henri ordered the Attorney-General to bring him to his *lever* next morning.

When, at six o'clock on Monday, the first of August, Clement heard Mass, he was overwhelmed by its appropriateness. The day was that of St. Peter ad Vincula and the Lesson told how St. Peter imprisoned by Herod was delivered by an angel, while the Gospel was the charter of the Catholic Church against heresy: 'Thou art Peter and it is upon this rock that I will build My church and the gates of Hell shall not prevail against it.' As an additional overtone, the Commemoration of the day was of the Maccabees, with the prayer: 'Lord, may the crown thou didst bestow upon the martyred brethren gladden us, bringing increase of virtue to those of us who believe and comforting us with their intercession.'

At eight o'clock, la Guesle, followed by Clement, after greeting the gentlemen-in-waiting in the ante-chamber of the royal bedroom, opened the door, only to discover that the King was not yet sufficiently dressed to grant an audience. Henri, however, ordered that the Attorney-General and the friar should be immediately introduced.

'*Mon frère*,' he said, 'what news from Paris?'

'M. le Premier Président is well and craves permission to kiss your hand.'

Clement then asked permission to speak privately to His Majesty. When La Guesle and du Halde, who was dressing Henri, demurred, the King himself commanded them to withdraw and pulled the friar to his side.

'What is it?'

'This,' said Clement, and, drawing the weapon from his sleeve, poniarded him in the stomach.

As Henri called out: 'The wretch has wounded me,' and wrenched the dagger from the wound, Clement turned his back and stood quietly with his arms outstretched in the form of a cross, waiting for the swords to thrust him through.

20

The End of the Valois

The King at first felt little pain, which gave some hope that the wound was not mortal. He dictated a letter to the Queen: 'God by His mercy so directed the blow that the wound is slight; and I hope in a few days to recover my accustomed health, in which trust I am encouraged, first, by my own feelings; secondly, by the opinion of my surgeons who believe that no danger exists. I have thought it wise to tell you of my true condition so that you may not be alarmed by false and contrary reports.' To this, he added a postscript in his own hand: 'M'Amye, I hope soon to be well. Pray God for me and do not leave the place where you now are.'

While he was writing it, Henry of Navarre came to his bedside. Henri stretched out his arms to him, saying: 'You see, brother, how my subjects have treated me! Be careful that they do not do the same to you!'

Navarre shed tears, as was expected; but this time—unexpectedly—the tears were genuine. He said nothing, but sat beside his brother-in-law, holding his hand, till the surgeons asked that space might be cleared round the bed for them to make further examinations. Under their ministrations Henri fainted with the pain. When he regained consciousness, he knew that he was dying.

More urgently now he spoke to Navarre: 'It is for you now to possess the Crown I have tried to preserve for you. Justice and the hereditary principle demand that you should succeed me; but I warn you, you will not keep the Crown—you may not even be able to wear it—unless you come back to the Church. You *must* change your religion. For your interest, as well as for your soul, you must become a Catholic again. Will you give me your word? Is not Paris worth a Mass?'

Navarre, ignoring the strangeness of such an appeal from one himself excommunicated, pointed out that he was already under instruction and would certainly submit at the proper time. Paris was certainly worth a Mass though he was not yet convinced that that was the price he would have to pay for it. King Henri might be dying, but the assault on Paris was still fixed for the morrow, and, in the inevitable victory, he should be able to impose his own terms.

Henri continued: 'May your reign be as fortunate as that of Charlemagne, our great ancestor! I will command all the servants of the Crown to take their oath of allegiance to you, now that you have promised to become a Catholic. You may still choose your own time but I have very little left and I should like to see it done before I go.'

All the nobles present then knelt and swore fidelity to the King of Navarre as the lawful inheritor of the Crown.

About two o'clock in the morning of August 2, the King, who, supported by Épernon and by the boy, Charles de Valois, the son of Charles IX and Marie Touchet, had been fitfully sleeping, woke with a start and, saying: 'The hour is at hand' called for his confessor. The priest, who had been waiting in the next room, came in hurriedly and before Henri could speak said: 'Sire, it is my miserable duty to remind you that unless you are determined to obey all the behests of our holy father, the Pope, as they are set forth in his admonition to you, I may not pronounce you absolved or give you the Blessed Sacrament.'

'It is my will and my intention,' said Henri, in a stronger voice than he had hitherto used, 'to satisfy His Holiness completely on every point.'

The priest then heard the King's confession, gave him absolution and administered the Last Sacraments.

Henri died in Épernon's arms at four o'clock on the morning of Wednesday 2 August 1589, the very hour at which the descent on Paris had been ordered to start.

D'Aubigné, the confidential friend of Henry of Navarre, left on record the scene in the Royal Bedroom when the new king returned to it: 'Henry IV found himself King sooner than he wished. Instead of acclamations of *Vive le roi!*, he beheld before him the corpse of his predecessor at whose feet knelt two monks holding lighted candles and reciting litanies. D'Entragues held the jaw of the deceased, while others wept, throwing themselves on the ground mumbling vows, prayers or protests. Some in this confusion fell on their knees and asked pardon for offences committed against the new king. To these the Duc d'Épernon said roughly: "Hold your tongues! You are like chattering women!" Others exclaimed quite close to the King's ear "that they would rather suffer ten thousand kinds of death than submit to a heretic prince!" The king, troubled at this, soon withdrew.'

The army disbanded. Swiss and Germans made haste to go home; what members of the French nobility there were, led by Épernon, retired with their retainers to their own provinces; even the Huguenots of the south deserted. In less than a week after Henri III's death, the army numbered less than 7,000 and all pretence of a siege of Paris was abandoned.

In the capital there were incredulous rejoicings. In the afternoon of August 2, the Duchess of Montpensier and her mother, the Duchess of Nemours, with Mayenne riding at their side, traversed the streets in a car drawn by six black horses, and announced: *'Bonne nouvelles! Le tyran est mort! Il n'y a plus de Henri de Valois en France!'* The churches were filled to overflowing for the *Te Deums* and lengthier thanksgivings. All the bells of the city were rung. On the following Sunday, August 7, Mayenne, as Lieutenant-General of the Kingdom, proclaimed the Cardinal de Bourbon, who was still a prisoner in Navarre's hands, King of France under the title of Charles X.

'Nothing was heard in Paris,' wrote a contemporary, 'but songs and rejoicing. The Duc de Mayenne and his followers assumed green scarfs and discarded the black which they had worn since the murders at Blois. Banquets, masquerades and shows were devised, during which the name of the deceased king was laden with curses and insults. The effigy of the "assassin-martyr" was carved in wood and painted on canvas and sold to decorate the houses of the Leaguers. He was invoked by many as a saint and martyr and his relatives were enriched by donations and public contributions.'

At St. Cloud, Navarre ordered that the dead and mutilated body of Clement was to be torn apart by wild horses, the remains burnt and the ashes scattered to the winds. One of the wits turned 'Frère Jacques Clement' into the anagram: '*C'est l'enfer qui m'a crée.*'

In Rome, the Pope, preaching before the Consistory of September 11, said, linking Clement with Judith: 'Such a holy, glorious and pious act could only have been inspired and executed by the immediate interposition of Almighty God. Our Almighty Lord, in thus saving miraculously the city of Paris also punished the iniquities committed by the deceased monarch of France. To Him, therefore, be ascribed glory and honour and, to the martyr Clement, the tribute of our veneration.'

Epilogue: St. James's Day 1593

Nearly four years passed before Navarre, on July 25 1593, St. James's Day—abjured Calvinism and heard Mass once more in Notre Dame. Those years saw the war at its bitterest with Henry unable to subdue the Catholic cause or to enter Paris even after a sixteen-weeks siege in which the privations were so great that, according to L'Estoile, the citizens were reduced to eating little balls of clay and slate which they mixed with water and swallowed. Mayenne's leadership might be uninspired but it was tenacious and it had the country behind it. Navarre was eventually forced to recognise that Calvinism, being such a minority religion, could never become the national creed of France and that only a Catholic king could be accepted by the whole nation. One of his young Huguenot followers, Rosny, told him: 'The counsel that you should go to Mass is one you cannot expect from me who am of the Reformed religion; nevertheless I will tell you there is no other way so speedy.'

The King was at last convinced that there was no other way at all. The Cardinal de Bourbon had died in 1590, leaving nothing but some 'Charles X' coinage and acts signed by him, and the States-General was about to appoint a young and energetic Prince of the Blood as his successor, which would ensure an endless civil war. Some Catholics were even prepared to call in Philip of Spain as 'Protector of the Realm' to counterbalance Henry's English, German and Swiss allies.

Above all, Gabrielle d'Estrées, Henry's new mistress—he had now tired completely of Corisande and neither saw nor wrote to her—was a Catholic who passionately urged him to abjure. The old Calvinist pastor Gabriel Damours dared say to him: 'If you would only listen, sire, to Gabriel Damours as you listen to Gabrielle, your *amour*, I should see you as a faithful king triumphing over your enemies. But I hear that you are ready to do what Solomon did when he turned to idolatry. It was a woman who urged him thereto.'

Henry replied: 'Prudence requires that I should be of the Catholic faith, not of yours, because in being of theirs I am saved both according to them and according to you, but, being of yours, I am only saved according to you, not according to them.'

On July 23, he wrote to Gabrielle: 'On Sunday I shall take the perilous leap' and, on the Sunday, reporting that he had made it: 'A pleasant adventure happened to me at church; an old woman of eighty seized me by the hair and kissed me. I joined in the laughter at it. Tomorrow you shall sweeten my mouth.'

He was received into the Church by the Archbishop of Bourges, having knelt to make his profession of faith outside the church and having renewed it at the altar when he received communion.[1] The day was dazzlingly hot; the citizens thronging the flower-strewn streets yelled themselves hoarse with

[1] Thereafter he remained not only a devout Catholic but a proselytising one.

Vive le roi! and in the evening the King sent a messenger to Madame de Montpensier to ask her, as one good Catholic to another, whether he might visit her for a game of cards.

She was too surprised to refuse and she laughed approvingly when he asked one of his Huguenot attendants: 'What do you say now seeing me installed in my good city of Paris?'

'I say, sire, that there is rendered to Caesar the things that are Caesar's.'

'*Ventre-Saint-Gris*,' said Henry IV, 'I have not been treated as Caesar, for nothing has been rendered to me but everything sold!'[2]

London
New Year's Day 1971

---

[2] It sounds better in French: '*On ne m'a rien rendu, mais tout vendu!*'

THE HOUSE OF FRANCE

LOUIS IX

(1) PHILIP III

JOHN

Charles

LOUIS XII

(2) Louis d'Orléans

John

Charles m. Louise of Savoy

FRANCIS I m. Claude

Margaret m. Henry d'Albret King of Navarre

HENRI II m. Catherine de Medici

Jeanne d'Albret Queen of Navarre

(1) Anthony de Bourbon

Francis d'Alencon (7)

Henry of Navarre m. Marguerite (6)

(5) HENRI III

(4) CHARLES IX m. Elizabeth of Austria

Claude (3) m. Charles Duke of Lorraine

Elizabeth (2) m. Philip of Spain

Mary of Scots m. FRANCIS II (1)

Mary m. James V of Scotland

(2) Robert de Bourbon

Francis de Bourbon

Antoinette m. Claude I Duke de Guise

Charles de Bourbon

(2) Charles Cardinal de Bourbon

(3) Louis I Prince de Condé

Henry I Prince de Condé

Charles Cardinal de Lorraine

Francis Duke de Guise "Le Balafré" m. Anne D'Este

Louis Cardinal de Lorraine

Henry I Duke de Guise

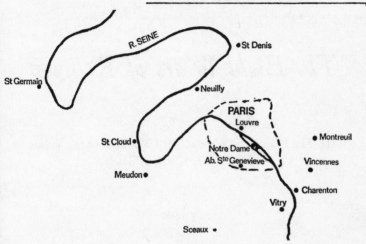

THE ENVIRONS OF PARIS

R. SEINE

• St Denis

St Germain •

• Neuilly

PARIS

Louvre

St Cloud •

• Montreuil

Notre Dame •
Ab. Ste Genevieve

Vincennes •

Meudon •

• Charenton

Vitry

Sceaux •

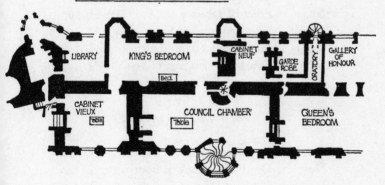

PLAN OF SECOND FLOOR OF BLOIS IN 1588

LIBRARY   KING'S BEDROOM   CABINET NEUF   GARDE ROBE.   ORATORY   GALLERY OF HONOUR

Bed.

CABINET VIEUX   Table   COUNCIL CHAMBER   Table   QUEEN'S BEDROOM

The Eight Wars of Religion

(I: The Florentine Woman II: The Last of the Valois
III: Paris is worth a Mass.)

Prelude

The First War 1562-63

Interlude

The Fourth War 1572-73

Interlude

The Fifth War 1574-76

Interlude 1576

The Sixth War 1577

The Eighth War 1585-89
(*The War of the Three Henries*)